11 POINTS GUIDE TO
HOOKING UP

11 POINTS GUIDE TO
HOOKING UP

LISTS AND ADVICE ABOUT FIRST DATES, HOTTIES, SCANDALS, PICKUPS, THREESOMES, AND BOOTY CALLS

SAM GREENSPAN

Skyhorse Publishing

Skyhorse Publishing books may be purchased in bulk at special discounts for sales promotion, corporate gifts, fund-raising, or educational purposes. Special editions can also be created to specifications. For details, contact the Special Sales Department, Skyhorse Publishing, 307 West 36th Street, 11th Floor, New York, NY 10018 or info@skyhorsepublishing.com.

www.skyhorsepublishing.com

10 9 8 7 6 5 4 3 2 1

Library of Congress Cataloging-in-Publication Data

Greenspan, Sam.
 11 points guide to hooking up : lists and advice about first dates, hotties, scandals, pickups, threesomes, and booty calls / by Sam Greenspan.
    p. cm.
 ISBN 978-1-61608-212-3 (pbk. : alk. paper)
 1. Dating (Social customs)--Humor. 2. Man-woman relationships--Humor. I. Title.
 PN6231.D3G736 2010
 818'.602--dc22

                    2010039349

Printed in China

Dedicated to Angie

For being the sole reason I have the credibility to write this book

Contents

Chapter Four:
SEX

Chapter Five:
DILEMMAS

Introduction

"**I** bet you have a bigger penis than Dr. Phil."

I paused and looked at my friend Nathan—my heterosexual, male friend Nathan. Of all the things in the world I thought he might say, *that* hadn't cracked the list. Nathan had never seen my penis (unless I've *really* blocked out something from college) and, I'm assuming, he'd never seen Dr. Phil's, either. But everyone has a different way of cheering people up, and it turns out this was his.

Rewind here for a second. For about five years, I worked at a job where I would go through countless dating, sex, and relationship books, magazine articles, and websites. And about two months in, I realized something: it felt like they were all saying the same thing. The same 50 or so pieces of advice get recycled, repackaged, and rewritten over, and over, and over. Primarily eye contact. You read enough of them and you get the feeling that if everyone would just make eye contact all the time we'd all be with our soul mates.

So last year, when my agent asked me how I wanted to turn my website into a book, my first instinct was: write a dating book. And not just any book. I wanted to write one that was completely fresh, one that didn't just regurgitate the same generic advice about making eye contact. Or eschewing a lame pickup line and just saying

"Hi." Or wearing a parrot on your shoulder to trick women into coming up and talking to you.

I spoke to several people in writing, publishing, and the literary world in general. "It's pretty much impossible to get a dating book published," one publishing veteran told me, "unless you're a big name, like Dr. Phil or Dr. Joyce Brothers. And even then it's tricky."

"Well, I have this website," I told him. "It's kinda popular. And people really seem to love it whenever I write about dating or sex up there. In fact, the most common suggestions and requests I get are for dating and sex lists. And when I write them, I think I'm putting something fresh out there into the world."

"Best of luck," he responded, essentially ending the conversation. "It's brutal out there."

And after that I played the waiting game—which is decidedly less fun than other games, like Hungry Hungry Hippos. Friends offered all kinds of support, from the more traditional "keep your head up" to the less traditional "I bet you have a bigger penis than Dr. Phil."

Obviously, since you're reading this in a book, there *was* one (gorgeous) publisher out there who agreed—with me, not about the Dr. Phil thing. So over the course of the summer of 2010, I spilled out every piece of dating, relationship, and sex advice; every anecdote, every experience, every theory I'd been storing in my comically oversized head. I spoke with dozens of people, from friends to strangers to therapists to (non-televised) doctors. I set out every day to write a guidebook to dating that would be different than any other book out there.

A little bit about how I ended up here. My name is Sam Greenspan. I'm 31 years old, I grew up in a suburb of Cleveland, Ohio, and now I live in Los Angeles. I've worked professionally as a writer since 2003. In 2008, I started a website called 11 Points, comprised entirely of 11-item lists. About a year later it developed a pretty great audience, which put me in a position to at least try to get a book off the ground. Since my blog didn't have one of those premises that just perfectly translate into a book—like "Cats Holding Ice Cream Cones" or "Crazy Things My Half-Vietnamese/Half-Inuit Parents Write on Facebook" or something—I had the opportunity to pitch this dating book.

I had my first girlfriend in fourth grade. I had my first real kiss in seventh. I had a girlfriend my senior year of high school and didn't have another one until I was 26. After we broke up two years later I went on a massive dating binge until I met my current girlfriend. Her name is Angie. She's gorgeous and funny and perfect in every way. (Note to my editor: If there are word count considerations, we can cut that line after she reads the rough draft. I doubt she'll read this again once it's printed.)

Before we dive in, I want to set up a few quick disclaimers and ground rules. First, I'm not a doctor or sex therapist. I don't have a degree in any medical or psychological field. I thought about getting a quick one from a diploma mill, but I doubt it would give more credence to this book if I were a PhD in sexology from the University of the Indian Ocean. My advice comes from actually being out there, actually trying everything—and from my irrepressible writer's instincts that somehow force me to observe and absorb every single detail I see.

Second, this book is written with an eye toward heterosexual couples. While I'm sure much of it could transfer over to homosexual couples, my observations here are based on my experience from the male-female dynamic. I don't know enough about the LGBT dating world to make informed statements—like, did you know surveys show lesbians are four to five times more likely than anyone else to have phone sex? I'm in way over my head. (I did watch five seasons of *The L Word*, which qualifies me for absolutely nothing . . . except the Leisha Hailey fan club. She's such a delightful lil' lady.)

And third, and most important, everything I wrote makes the baseline assumption that, deep down, you're a good person; that you don't get off on hurting or manipulating people; that you sometimes get nervous before dates; that your endgame on dates isn't *always* just a free meal or free intercourse. This isn't just a handbook on tricks to get laid or tricks to getting married within the calendar year. These are real, grounded ideas targeted at real, grounded human beings.

So that's the deal. I hope you find the ideas in this book to be hilarious, eye-opening, and ingenious. Although if you just occasionally chuckle, find about one-11th of the advice to be useful, and consider the book to be "kinda interesting," I'll call that a victory, too. After all, I've got you reading a book. And you don't even get a free personal pan pizza from BOOK IT! for finishing it.

One final note, as much as my friend was trying to cheer me up in my troubled quest to get a dating advice book to market, I really don't think I have a bigger penis than Dr. Phil. I'm a 5-foot-8 Jewish guy. He's a 7-foot-3 Southerner who's built like an offensive lineman who ate another offensive lineman.

But I bet I have a bigger penis than Dr. Joyce Brothers.

Probably.

11 POINTS GUIDE TO
HOOKING
UP

1

Meeting

Damn, I wish I was a black guy.

    As I stood there, alone, at a nightclub in Las Vegas that was the first thought that ran through my mind. (My second thought was: "Or is the correct grammar, 'Damn, I wish I *were* a black guy'?") I nervously sucked down an $8 Bud Light because I needed some-thing—anything—to do besides awkwardly cling to the wall, staring out at all the people dancing, like one of the nerds in an eighties movie wearing ruffled tuxes and thinking they have a shot at Molly Ringwald.

    I love a good, under-the-radar stereotype, and here's one of the best: Somehow, it seems, black guys just don't have that same fear of rejection that's crippled me for oh-so-many years.[1]

    Of course, it's not true across the board—I've had many shy black friends and, ya know, there's a cowardly lion in *The Wiz*—but damn if I haven't seen the scene play out too many times to count. A black guy, not necessarily good looking or charismatic—in fact,

---

[1]   Other good under-the-radar stereotypes: Women only use one password for every website, Jews don't drink milk with dinner, and all Goth kids weigh either under 115 or over 220 pounds.

often, neither—walks up to a random girl, confidently takes her arm, gets her attention, and says some secret, magical phrase to her.[2] Odds are, she rejects him. Wholly unfazed, he takes two steps over to another girl, confidently takes her arm, gets her attention, and repeats the process. This particular night in Vegas I watched this one guy work that routine with nine different girls until I finally lost sight of him in the crowd.

Let's contrast *that* scene with what happened to me, just moments before. I'd seen a girl I thought was cute about a half hour earlier, while I was taking a lap around the club. She was with a large bachelorette party. I didn't say anything then, just raised my eyebrows in her direction and kept walking. Now, 30 minutes and zero women talked to later, I saw her again, this time on the dance floor. I decided that, this time, I'd try to say something clever.

And that clever phrase turned out to be . . . "Who's the bride?" Not poetry by any means. But, in my mind, I figured that'd be a good enough "in" to start talking to her, and if she was at all attracted to me, we'd be fine from there. After all, it was Vegas. Everyone gives you a little more leeway there than in real life.[3]

"Her," she said, pointing at the girl wearing the tiara and the sash reading "Bride-to-be." "Oh, I figured she'd won the Miss USA pageant or something," I hilariously replied. "So where are you guys from?" "Hold on a sec," she replied, then turned around and started dancing with a few of her friends. I spent about eight excruciating seconds standing there like a lost child before turning around and walking the other direction, trying (and failing) to look cool.

---

[2] A few years ago, I was making a Web video where I was interviewing random people on Bourbon Street in New Orleans and asked a black guy about this. He said the secret phrase is "Hey, pretty girl." No other person would confirm or deny, so it remains my best guess.

[3] There'll be a lot more about this phenomenon later in Chapter 4, in the "11 Places You Can Be Sexually Casual without Judgment" list.

I retreated against the wall for a while, eventually met back up with a few friends, and ended up leaving the club to gamble within an hour. I would not say a word to another woman that night.[4]

I can describe that scene in vivid detail because, to this day, every rejection I've experienced, however nominal, still sticks with me.

I was an extraordinarily shy child, I'm an only child who hates confrontation, and I'm a former fat guy who still has self-esteem scars that burn like a Harry Potter plot device. All of those have collaborated to ensure every single rejection I endure is crippling.

That's when I think of the black guy, who, in about four minutes, was rejected the same number of times that I've been rejected in 10 years. And who probably kept on going until he finally found that one in 50, one in 100, who thought he was good looking or found his compliment genuine.

I'm an extreme case, for sure . . . but not *that* extreme. I have extremely confident friends, confrontational ones, ones who weren't only children, ones who were never fat—all of whom are just as petrified of female rejection as I am. And when it comes to my female friends . . . from what I've observed, if a woman breaks from society's natural order, hits on a guy, and he rejects her, she'll downward spiral into a self-loathing shell even quicker.

Which brings us to the thesis of this entire chapter of the book: Trying to pick up and meet new people is soul-wrenchingly awful (unless you're a non-shy black guy).[5]

But it's something you have to do. It's a 100 percent necessity if you're going to live a single life that's not lonely, boring, and wasted.

---

[4] Other than the elderly female Korean blackjack dealer who reminded me that when an elderly female Korean blackjack dealer has a six showing, there's a 99.3 percent chance her hole card is a five.

[5] I joke about this, but I fully recognize there are plenty of black guys out there who don't have that natural outgoingness. I'm Jewish, and it took me until age 30 to get my credit score into the 800s. Every stereotype has its outliers.

Because *that* single life is soul-wrenchingly awful in a different, and ultimately much worse, way.

This chapter is devoted to overcoming the fear of rejection that festers inside you; finding the confidence, strength, and extroversion necessary to colonic it right out. (Figuratively, of course. At least I hope figuratively.)

It's not about tricks, like going to a club wearing a purple fur coat, a T-shirt that says "Certified Vagologist," a Mickey Mouse nose ring, mismatched combat boots, a monocle, and a snake wrapped around your neck, all in the grotesquely desperate hope that some girl will approach you and ask about one of them . . . only so you can reply, "I'm surprised someone who looks as dumb as you would think to ask a question like that!"

It's not about mantras to repeat to yourself in the mirror ("I'll never see any of these people again, don't hesitate, make a move"), which ultimately won't do a damn thing for you when you're in the moment, thinking about approaching someone, and suddenly you get overtaken by the dormant shy kid inside you who used to hide behind his/her mom because the Chuck E. Cheese characters were too scary.

This chapter is about real, tested, smart ways to get yourself out there, so you can meet the people you want to meet, date the people you want to date, and maybe, just maybe, channel your inner outgoing, fearless, enviable, confident black guy to ease on down the road of unprecedented dating success.

11 Bar and Party Pickup Strategies That Actually Work

It's quite sad that pickup lines are a dead art because everyone—*everyone*—loves pickup lines. I bet one of the first 11 homemade Web pages was a list of horrible pickup lines.[6] But now, everyone knows you don't walk up to someone at a bar and give some hackneyed line. ("What's the difference between your legs and my low-budget independent film? I'm going to find a way to get your legs to open wide.")

Those are out. Tragically. The ideas in this list are not. They come from the trial and error of my friends, acquaintances, newly divorced coworkers (of both genders), and me, overcoming any inner cowardice to talk to, pick up and, sometimes, take home strangers at bars and parties.

(1) Talk in the bathroom line. I always hate trying to use my charm (for whatever it's worth) on a dance floor. Walking up to someone who's dancing, getting in personal space–violating proximity to his/her ear and trying to yell "HEY, WHAT'S YOUR NAME?" over some DJ blasting a 150-decibel Avril Lavigne–Thin Lizzy mash-up.[7]

That's why I love the bathroom line. Most times, the men's and women's bathrooms are close to each other, or even shared. It's away from the chaos, and far enough away from the music that you can talk at a more reasonable volume. Plus, *you have a conversation starter that, when properly delivered, doesn't feel*

---

[6]   Quite possibly on a web page with a starry background and an animated dancing 7UP Spot.

[7]   "The Sk8er Bois Are Back in 2wn."

badly clichéd: make a quick joke about how men aren't supposed to have to wait in bathroom lines.

Eventually, you'll both use the bathroom and go your separate ways—but now, you can try to find the person again, and easily have an in.[8]

(2) Casual teasing that lets your "good person" show through. Seduction books for guys say, basically, that you have to act more dickish than William Zabka to pick up women. You're supposed to walk up to a group of people, find the girl you like, say to one of her friends, "Hey, why do you hang out with this *bitch*!?" and then put up your hand for a high five.

That's ridiculous. I assume you want to meet people/hook up/ date as a real human being and not some kind of caricature. You can and should do that with your real, likable, Ralph Macchio–esque personality.

That being said, you (both men and women) do need some level of teasing. Don't lob aggressive insults,[9] but show that you've got some edge, that you'll call him/her out on bullshit, that you're going to have fun together—and that *you're a good person who's being funny, not malicious.*

(3) Venture out wingman-free. A wingman can be great, but if things aren't working, break off solo. I look at it as a math equation. (I look at a lot of things as math equations. We'll just call that part of my charm.)

Let's say if I talk to a random girl, there's a 25 percent chance she'll be receptive. If I'm with a wingman and we approach two girls, we're now each bringing our one-in-four chance with us. Meaning

---

[8] Plus, if there was a bathroom attendant, you just spent $1 to get a mint, which should make the conversation much smoother. If it was a house party, you didn't get a mint, but you DID get to rifle through a stranger's medicine cabinet and see their fungal creams, and that'll get anyone's adrenaline pumping—which is also good for this situation.

[9] Like, "Hey, is your dad dead? Because if I had a daughter that ugly I'd murder my wife, then kill myself! You wanna grab some coffee this week?"

that, if we've both targeted one of the girls, there's only a one-in-16 chance that each of them is going to be receptive to each of us. In other words, *you're the anti-Voltron*—when you guys combine powers, instead of making an awesome megarobot (that in no way rips off *Transformers*), your combo often makes you far less attractive to girls.

Quite possibly as unattractive as someone who talks about Voltron.

(4) But . . . if your friend is outnumbered, jump in. It almost feels like cheating. But if you see one of your friends has successfully broken through to a group, go ahead and barge right on in. In theory, *he/she will introduce you and you can pick off someone from the group to focus on*—just *not* the person your friend wants. That's incredibly dirty. It's like when the Goonies did all the work to find One-Eyed Willie's treasure, then the Fratellis tried to swoop in at the end and steal it. And what happened to them? Jail. Think about that.

(5) Approaching a group with the right ratio. This isn't to say you won't have success conquering larger groups. But trying to pick someone up with all their friends watching is like trying to sell magazines by approaching a huge crowd and yelling, "Hey, any of you assholes want to buy a subscription to *Women's Day*?" instead of doing it the smart way that ex-cons have perfected: by walking door-to-door and getting people one-on-one.

I've found that there are two absolutely sweet situations that vastly skew the percentages in your favor:[10] (1) Two friends, where

---

[10] It's like in poker. Yes, if you're dealt a three and a seven you might end up with a straight. But it's far more likely that any money you put in is going to be scooped up by the 78-year-old Vietnamese guy with an eye patch across the table who started the hand with a pair of kings. For those keeping score at home—and if you're keeping score while reading a book, you may not fully comprehend how the concept of "score" works—I'm about three pages into the book and have now dropped stereotypes on blacks, Jews, Goth kids, Koreans, and Vietnamese. I'm the Don Rickles of people with hot pink books.

one of them is talking with someone and the other one is trying to look cool but is clearly frantically uncomfortable as a third wheel. Or, (2) one person, solo. In both scenarios, *you get a receptive audience from someone who's basically solo* like you . . . and secretly praying you'll head over and strike up some riveting bar conversation.

(6) Harness the awesome power of the callback. I love callback humor. I love it as much as the Voltron force loved protecting the planet Arus. And I've found that callbacks ended up being a very effective pickup strategy.

As you're doing a lap of the bar or party, make a few brief, joke-ish comments to a few attractive people. They don't have to be good jokes (thus "joke-*ish*"). If someone's pounding a drink, even something as generic as "Whoa, slow down" is fine. Make sure it's in passing; after you make the joke, keep walking.

Later, on a future lap, when you see that person, reference what you said: "Hey, it's Chugging Guy." In theory this shouldn't work. You've now made two "jokes" that, out of context, even the über-forgiving *Married . . . With Children* laugh track wouldn't respond to. And that thing will howl at anything. But somehow . . . the person will almost definitely respond with a laugh, a smile, and a "Hey!" right back to you.

You're establishing a friendly familiarity without actually being friends or familiar. Even with two mediocre faux-jokes you've established a recurring connection. Callbacks are just that powerful.[11]

(7) Order an interesting drink when you want to get the attention of the person standing next to you. The following drinks are not conversation starters: any well-known brand of beer,

---

[11]   More powerful than the fungal cream you'd find in someone's medicine cabinet.

vodka and anything, rum and anything, gin and tonic, whiskey and Coke, margarita, generic wines, soda, or water.

The following drinks *are* conversation starters: weirdly named shots, Jägermeister, anything that involves the word "bomb," Scotch (assuming you can spout off a bunch of Scotch terms), *anything that comes in a fishbowl or oversized goblet,* a non-generic martini, something where you ask for more than four lime wedges or nine olives, or anything that includes cucumber.

(8) Approach with a 10-second "out." Might as well soften the blow if you get brutally rejected. When you approach someone, *treat it like a drive-by*—talk to him/her on your way to somewhere (the bar, the bathroom, your friends, whatever).

You're going to say something. Within seconds, you'll know if he/she is receptive, or going to blow you off.[12] In the first case, you'll stop and talk. In the second case, keep walking the hell away from there.

(9) Outside. Outside a bar or party is so tranquil. *It's like a koi pond that's filled with drunken, human koi.* The party becomes like a little insular bubble where your interactions are magnified and scrutinized in an overheated crucible. When you step outside to the fresh (or, if you're a smoker, completely and totally unfresh) air, it's not just a physical separation from the party, it's a mental one as well.

(10) Compliment a woman with a quick, genuine statement about her attractiveness relative to the other women in the room. It's uncanny—women have an incredible ability to walk into a room and instantly know where they rank, attractive-

---

[12] It always kills me how adding "off" to the end of that sentence causes such an 180 in its meaning.

ness-wise, versus every other female there. It's the gender's universal superpower.[13]

Your angle? *Let her know that she's ranking herself too low.* You have to say something that's not over the top (which makes it seem like you're just fraudulently flattering her), and you have to say it with conviction. Leaning in and saying, "I just wanted to let you know I think you're the best-looking girl in here" is probably going to work. Even if she *believes* deep down that's not true, you saying that just changed her night.

And then, follow it up with some casual teasing like, "But, really, in the bottom five when it comes to dancing."

(11) Compliment a guy on his clothing. A guy has confidence about his looks—how he did his hair, his ability to be incredibly hilarious. But he *knows you understand fashion far better than he,* so any validation of his clothing really stands out.

I was going to relay an anecdote here about when I was at a club a few years ago, and a girl came up and complimented the tie I was wearing. But instead, I'll talk about the time at a seventh-grade dance when a girl complimented the silk shirt I was wearing. (It was the early nineties. Color Me Badd was dictating fashion.) I still remember that two decades later. Now *that's* a powerful compliment.

But, no, as a seventh grader, I did not sex her up.

---

[13]   The male gender's superpower? The ability to get three months' wear out of a pair of jeans without washing them.

11 Strategies for Increasing Your
Online Dating Success

Your photos are, by far, the number one reason someone's going to check out your profile. I'd guess they're around 75 percent. So if those photos aren't good, none of this matters. But assuming you've put your best pictures forward, hopefully these strategies can help you nail that other quarter, too.[14]

(1) Only sign up for one site—and pick a major one. Online dating is more time-consuming than playing Risk *and* sitting through your nephew's third-grade recorder recital. So pick one major dating site (to give you the most potential matches), clear off your calendar, and get ready to take on a second full-time job.[15]

Beyond the time commitment, it's good to pick just one site because *you don't want to be pegged as a serial online dater.* The standard mission statement of an online dater is: "I've heard so much I finally decided to try this out." You can't cite the "try this out" hedge if you're signed up for 15 sites.

(2) Look like your photos. I know you looked amazing when you were 18, in great shape, tan, and filled with the bright-eyed happiness that disappears once you have to figure out how to get your own health insurance. But, if that photo doesn't look anything

---

[14] And if you want photo help, check out the list in Chapter 4 called "11 Secrets for Taking Fantastic Nude Photos" . . . and go through with a pen crossing out "nude" and writing in "online dating." It works on like nine of the 11 points on that list.

[15] Assuming your employer doesn't block your site, this second full-time job will most definitely interfere with your current full-time job.

like you today, you'll get a lot of first dates but virtually no second dates—because it's doubly sabotaging you.[16]

Not only will the person be a little disappointed when he/she sees you . . . *no amount of sparkling personality can overcome the fact that you pulled a bait-and-switch.*

So pick recent photos where you look good—no need to choose the one taken from below that gives you 14 chins and spooky, cavernous nostrils just for the sake of over-honesty—and make sure the person isn't going to see you and think, "Wait . . . really?"

(3) Avoid clichés like the plague. You're putting together an online dating profile, not the screenplay to a *Sex and the City* movie. So you're not putting your best foot forward *or* giving 110 percent if you say any of these: "I love getting dressed up for a big night out, but I also love getting pizza and watching a DVD"; "I can't believe I am doing this, but here I am"; "I'm looking for someone with a *great sense of humor who doesn't play games.*"

(4) . . . except for the one cliché that's really good. There's only one cliché I can advocate. Use a line like, "And even though we're meeting online, we can just tell everyone we met through friends or when you rescued me from a burning building or something."

It's great because it accomplishes three major goals: (1) *It addresses everyone's insecurities about the residual online dating stigma,* (2) it shows your sense of humor, (3) *and* it gives people a layup for something funny to write in a message to you. ("Yeah, I'm totally into saying we met as arson suspects!")

---

[16]   Also, don't just slap up a photo of Gordie Howe.

(5) Show, don't tell. Phrases like, "I'm low maintenance," "I'm adventurous," or worst of all, "I'm really funny," are almost always signs that you're high maintenance, boring, or as funny as awards show banter, respectively.

Use examples to illustrate yourself. Instead of "I'm low maintenance," try "I can't ever get famous because the paparazzi would get daily photos of me wearing sweatpants and getting drive-thru at Wendy's." Instead of "I'm adventurous," put up a photo from your last time rock climbing or BASE jumping or riding on the back of Falkor. Instead of "I'm really funny" . . . ya know, write something funny.

(6) Fill in the blanks. If you leave blanks for the questions about *body type, height, have kids, want kids, or smoking,* it looks like you have something to hide. (Up to and including the thought that you might be a voluptuous 8-footer with three kids who smokes two packs a day.)

(7) Be picky about being picky. It's *a fine line between knowing what you want and looking either narrow-minded or desperate.* If you say you want a woman 18 or 19 only, that sends a message. If you're looking for someone 18 to 64, that sends a *really* different message. If you're only looking for men who are over 6-foot-3 with an athletic body type, expect to see your potential options plummet.[17]

Err on the side of a more generous range for most categories—and be as specific as you want on the *one* big area that matters most to you. Maybe it's a Catholic guy, or a red-haired girl, or you have

---

[17] Especially on JDate.

a fetish for men who are exactly 5-foot-8.[18] Be a little more picky there, and a little more generous elsewhere.

(8) Be smart about your username. Avoid *something that's a red flag in and of itself*—words like player, hunter, pussy, wife, balls, grrl, sleepless, seattle, carriebradshaw, notcrazy, actor, actress, heigl, diva, battlestar, hopelessromantic, hopefulromantic, areola, or cougar.[19]

I think the best usernames contain a semi-obscure TV, movie, or music reference. Make it something that won't seem too strange to people who don't get it . . . and, if someone does get it and is also a fan, he or she will instantly vault you to the top of the list because of your clear compatibility.[20]

(9) Be selective about who you go out with. Just like you don't go out with every person who winks at you in real life, you don't have to go out with everyone who e-winks at you in fake life. Treat it like a buffet—*eat the prime rib, crab legs, and éclairs; don't waste precious space on useless filler like salad or fruit.*

(10) Read date cancellations as a sign. Odds are you're getting a lot of dating opportunities, and you're developing a thought process of "well, if this one gets away, there's always another one."

Lots of online dates seem to get canceled the day of. Subconsciously, you're prioritizing dates—and if you're not genuinely excited about the date, you won't have a problem canceling it for whatever's come up, big (work event, medical emergency, mauled by a bear) or small (headache, no clean clothes, mauled by a fish).

---

[18] In my experience, this fetish does not exist. But I keep dreaming.

[19] Either referring to the fact that you're an older woman who likes younger guys or that you support Washington State University athletics. Both can be red flags.

[20] A friend of mine went out with a guy solely because his Match.com name was BluthBananas. And rightfully so.

With a cancellation you've lost 90 percent of the already-tenuous momentum you had to begin with. After a second cancellation, you might as well euthanize the date, because it's clear there's not enough mutual enthusiasm to make it work.

(11) Get the paid membership. It's simple. If I'm paying for online dating and you're not, you make me look like a sucker who's *way* more desperate than you.

Here's the secret for getting your membership for free. Call your mom. Tell her you've decided you want to meet someone (who, of course, is of the religious/ethnic slant she lusts for) and you want to sign up for online dating . . . but gosh darnit it's expensive. The $60 check will be in the mail before you've even reached the part of the phone call where she talks for 10 minutes about how muggy it is outside.

11 Best Ways to

Hook Up on Vacation

Vacation operates under a different set of rules than real life. You're freer, happier, and more open-minded when you don't have to do laundry, eat a meal-replacement bar for breakfast, or sit in two-hour meetings so your boss can remind everyone to always consider "Is this good for the company?"

(1) Pick a strategic place to go. While, yes, you can hook up no matter where you go—there's probably even someone in Vatican City right now who'd be happy to commit some sins with you—choosing the right place will boost your chances. *Backpacking through Europe, a Caribbean cruise,* a ski trip, or finding a tour group that specializes in your age-group—these are vacations where your odds of hooking up will be . . . well, I was going to say "looking up" but that treads dangerously close to Dr. Seuss territory.

(2) Spend some time going where the locals go. Tourist-on-tourist hookups are fine—but locals are the sweet spot. If you go to Italy, you don't want to go home and tell people you had a wild sexual adventure with a guy who was there visiting from Raleigh. You want to talk about your weeklong fling with a dark-haired, olive-skinned winemaker named Sergio.[21]

The best way to do this is to *go where the locals go.* Ignore the guidebooks, use the Internet, and explore. You're pretty much guaranteed to stand out from the crowd, and locals will be surprisingly inclined to approach you. It makes sense—they know you're

---

[21] I mean—I'm hetero, and I kinda want to have a weeklong fling with Sergio.

there for an adventure, that you won't be bitchy to them, and that you'll be legitimately excited to talk.[22]

(3) Spend at least some of your vacation solo. The reason is simple: It will absolutely force you to meet people (plus, you know, all that pabulum about really getting to know yourself). *If you don't dust off your social skills, you're going to be alone.* That alone should, at the very minimum, put you in a position to find someone to hook up with.[23]

(4) Be my tour guide? If he/she likes you, being your unpaid tour guide won't be a burden. It's win-win. You'll get to see some of the best spots . . . he/she gets to be your revered, respected expert . . . and *you both get to live out the local expert/wide-eyed traveler fantasy.*

You know those movie montages where two people are running around in a country taking pictures, splashing in a fountain, sitting in a park, marveling at sculptures, eating local cuisine, and laughing in each others' arms in front of legendary landmarks that somehow miraculously aren't overcrowded with gawking tourists? This is your montage. (Of course, if you really did all those things you'd be exhausted, your feet would explode, and you *would* be lost in a sea of other, more boorish tourists, but, again, your logical mind is getting in the way right now.)

(5) If you're still at the hostel age, stay in hostels. As far as I'm concerned, *if you are or appear to be under 39 years old, you should stay at hostels.* If the movie *Hostel* taught me anything, it's that, when you get to your room, there will be gorgeous, naked, promiscuous Slovakian models eagerly waiting

---

[22] I experience this in L.A. a lot, where we have tourists year-round—you can always find the visitors, whether by their accents, their wide-eyed confusion, or the fact that they're wearing shorts because they can't believe it's 62 degrees in February. And, within about 20 minutes of being at a bar, people are always chatting them up.

[23] And yes, it also puts you in a position to be abducted. We'll cover that more in point 7.

for you. (I only watched the first 15 minutes of the movie. I assume nothing bad transpired after that.)

(6) Keep your agenda loose. You *don't want to miss out on the night of your life because you have to wake up* at 5:45 AM to get in line for an all-day bus tour of the historic doors of Lisbon. (At the same time, you don't want to miss out on that tour because you refused to mercy kill a night that needed to be mercy killed, and you stayed at a club until 5:45 AM vainly hoping that you'd find a Portuguese lover there among the scraps. Those historic doors are probably kinda cool, after all.)

(7) Don't drop your usual vetting process just because you're away from home. A sobering moment, briefly, to talk safety. You're in a strange place, about to put an inordinate amount of trust in a strange person. While most likely only good things are about to happen—you just never know. *Don't let the zeal of your fantasy obstruct your usual precautionary measures*—make sure you pay attention to where he/she is taking you, that you have your phone with you and emergency numbers handy, that you told *someone* your plan for the night, and that you don't see a book called *Trafficking Human Organs for Fun and Profit* in the back-seat of his/her Peugeot.

(8) Use condoms (even weird-looking foreign ones). I know that your fantasy of passionate vacation sex in a small cottage overlooking a field of windmills and tulips in Holland doesn't include a 90-second break to put on a strange-smelling Dutch condom. I know. But *flings require condoms.* Syphilis doesn't care what country you're in.[24]

---

[24] Also, when you're filling out your customs form on the way home, you really don't want to have to debate whether or not to declare the penicillin you got at a Dutch pharmacy.

(9) Don't burden yourself with expectations. Not gonna lie, after reading all of the above, super high hookup expectations might be my fault. But remember: like all things in life, *high expectations are the best way to guarantee disappointment.*[25] So plan a vacation that sounds like it'll be a blast whether *or not* you hook up.

If you do hinge everything on hooking up, you'll find yourself getting by turns depressed and desperate—both of which will actually make it far *more* difficult for you to find someone.

(10) Never scare off someone by telling him you're trying to get your groove back. No handsome, muscular island man-boy will just give you your groove back. *He's only got so much groove* to dispense to groove-strapped older women. If he knows you're in it for the groove, he'll probably be in it for the money.

(11) Leave vacation romance on vacation. This is by far the most important point on this list. So go ahead and forget everything else and just remember this. Yes, there is an outside chance that you're going to have a vacation romance with the person who turns out to be your true soul mate, one and only, blah, blah, blah.

The problem is: *Your romance isn't real.* It exists in a hyperspeed vacuum. You're both going in knowing that you've got a shelf life of, what, a week, maybe 10 days? You're going to compress everything into that window. It's accelerated, it's a whirlwind, and it's fantasy. You very well may have the best week of your life, and the memories will be incredible.

But they need to stay on vacation. If you go back and visit again, or, even more seriously, one of you moves to the other's city . . . it

---

[25] Fittingly, it's like when I went to see the movie *EuroTrip* in the theater. I had ultralow expectations, so I was pleasantly surprised. Treat your Euro trip like I treated *EuroTrip*.

will never be the same. Nothing will ever compare to when you were strangers that week. The memories will be tarnished the second time around, when reality sets in, the whirlwind is over, and you actually get to know each other.[26]

---

[26] This happened to me a few years back after I met someone in Vegas. We had one tremendously exciting night. She lived in L.A., and, a few weeks later, we got together back at home. It was disastrous. Nothing was the same. We had no chemistry. Our date was insanely awkward. We never spoke again after that night. We didn't have a vacation romance— romance is *definitely* not the right word for it—but we did have a vacation connection. A fraudulent, one-night-only, drunken Vegas connection. I was also told during my last round of revisions that this concept is the basis for the movie *Forget Paris*. I'm proud not to have known that.

11 Reasons You Keep Going Out but Aren't Meeting Anyone

Everyone goes through droughts. Dating seems to go in cycles—sometimes your roster of prospects is full, sometimes it's empty. Full is a good problem. Empty is when you start to wonder if anyone will ever love you again, and if it's time to start looking up mail-order brides (for men) or moving to an Alaskan logging town where the ratio is 475:1 (for women). I've actually witnessed people do both. [27]

And when you're going out two, three, five nights a week and not meeting any good people to date, that's when the droughts get droughtier. [28]

This list is your slump breaker. All 11 of these probably won't apply to you—unless you're more socially awkward than the love child of Michael Scott and Franklin D. Asperger, which would make you the most socially awkward person in the world (and you're not, because I know definitively that Keanu Reeves is). But as you read through this list, you very well may see one or two things that make you think, "Hey, ya know, I really might be sabotaging myself by doing that. Whoa."

(1) You read as "unapproachable." As I walk through a social event—bar, party, barbecue, Quinceañera, ice cream social, church picnic I'm crashing because I just know I can win the $15 Long John Silver's gift card for first prize in the egg-spoon carry—I

---

[27] Really. My friend Gabe had a female coworker who decided to pack up and move to Alaska because she went there for a marathon and had hundreds of men hit on her. As for the mail-order bride, I've been asked not to use that person's name or story.

[28] Because I just used "droughtier" in a book, I think that officially starts the process of making it a real word.

instinctively find myself sizing up every woman's approachability. And I'm always surprised at how many are sending off "stay the hell away from me" signs (and not just at the church picnic).

Here's a quick list within a list[29] of things you might be doing that are unapproachable: your arms are folded; you keep glancing at your watch or cell phone to see what time it is; you rudely dismiss someone who tried to talk to you; you roll your eyes at people; you're the only person wearing your jacket; you're positioned at a table where you have people on both sides; *you're with a coed group and it's hard to tell if you're single or with someone;* you have a look of fear in your eye; you don't reciprocate when people smile at you; your friends look bored; you never wander off alone from your friends.

(2) You keep going to the same places. We get into routines. Unless you're a spy or, even less likely, a working actor, there's a damn good chance that each day is fairly similar. It happens with your social life, too. You find that *you and your friends mostly go to the same handful of nearby bars, to parties where you see the same people,* and to church picnics with the same egg-spoon-race contestants.[30]

You're in a dating slump because you're in a social slump that's just reinforcing the same patterns of slumpification. So . . . uh . . . try switching things up. Find a new place to go, in a new part of town. Go out with a different group of people—even if it's got to be the coworkers who are perfect "work friends" but you never really thought you'd hang out with. Stop instantly deleting your daily barrage of Facebook event invitations and actually check out a random "friend" playing live music.

---

[29] It's like the play within a play in *Hamlet.* Or as they said on *The Simpsons,* like watching home movies of you watching TV.

[30] In other words, even in a music video you'd see the same hoes.

(3) You're going out with too many couples. *Couples have agendas.*[31] Even the world's funnest couple doesn't have that energy that comes from being a single person on the hunt.

(4) You're *too* nice to everyone you meet. A good female friend of mine has this problem. When we go out, she's extraordinarily nice to every guy she talks to—whether she wants to ravish him right there against the Golden Tee machine or she wants to bash his head into the PhotoHunt machine.[32] And the result of this undying kindness is . . . guys are apprehensive about asking her out.

People don't like rejection. If I'm talking to you and getting a good read that you're interested, but then I watch you give the exact same level of attention to every other guy you talk to, I start doubting that you were really interested in me. If you like someone, *you need to give him/her more attention, flirtation, and signs than you give everyone else.*

(5) You come off as rehearsed. It's easy to read when someone's going through the motions with you, when you're talking to him/her and just hearing a list of standard, generic questions— "Where do you work? Where did you grow up? Do you call it pop or soda? What's the deal with airline food?"[33]

The best way to show someone that you have genuine interest is to . . . ready for it? . . . *actually take a genuine interest.* This comes from letting the conversation flow naturally, listening to the answers you get, and asking follow-up questions.

(6) You need to refresh your look. I don't follow fashion trends closely, but I do know this: When your hair is done right, and

---

[31] Often, the agenda is putting in enough time out to qualify as "still fun" . . . then getting home by one at the latest. If they've been together for eight months or less, it's to have sex. If they're been together longer than that, it's to get a really good night's sleep.

[32] She goes to a lot of bars that have video games. Apparently.

[33] If you're a throwback kind of person, feel free to add "What's your sign?" "You party?" and "Got any 'ludes?" to that list.

you're wearing a new shirt that fits really well, *you're going to have a better night than usual.*

This goes back to the stagnation idea. If you're not just going to the same places and seeing the same people, but you're wearing the same old clothes and same old hairstyle every time, too, you've hit a double rut—which is the second deadliest kind of rut. (Not as bad as the triple rut though—same places, same clothes/hair, same ex you call and text all night when you don't find someone to flirt with within seven minutes.)

(7) You're going out too much. This piece of advice will work in opposition to every other book or article ever written on dating. So take that, famous peoples' ghostwriters. If you're going out every single night, you're taking the pressure off yourself. If you don't talk to anyone tonight, it's fine—you'll get 'em tomorrow.

One way to light a fire under yourself is to slash and burn your number of opportunities. If you're only going out one night this week, you damn well better be bolder, braver, and more outgoing that night, because if you don't, you'll have another dateless week.

It's like in *Rudy*—he got in for one play in his entire college football career, and he sacked the quarterback, 'cause he wasn't going to blow that opportunity. Meanwhile, in *Air Bud: Golden Receiver*, that dog gets so many reps that it doesn't matter if he catches the ball or not, he knows he's always got the next play to make something happen. You want to be Rudy, not Air Bud.

(8) You're misinterpreting the signs you're getting. You're having a million conversations but no dates. You can't tell if people like you or they're just killing time talking with you.

Here's a good test: Find a way to mention a place you've always wanted to go—a restaurant, a museum, a new bar, a part of town named after an ethnicity (Chinatown, Little Italy, Wee Britain, Irelandland). If the person's interested in you, *he/she will grab that opportunity* to say something like, "I've always wanted to go there, too," or, more to the point, "We should go together." And the next thing you know, you, my friend, have a date to visit China-town.[34]

(9) You're waiting for people to come to you. Yes, rather than actively approaching and talking to people, *it's infinitely easier to just sit there and have a steady stream of strangers come up and hit on you all night.* It's also easier to quit your job and make a billion dollars by helping an exiled Zambian prince transfer his fortune to a bank account in England.[35] But that's not a sound strategy for success, either.

If you're a guy, and you're not famous or over 6-foot-8, nine times out of 11 you're going to need to initiate things. If you're a woman, you can absolutely sit there and get hit on . . . but if you have your eye on someone in particular, you can make *sure* he talks to you by actually approaching him first.[36]

(10) You aren't experimenting with new places to go. When I was 21, if you'd asked me to rank where I thought I'd pick up the most girls over the next decade, I would've said, from most to least: parties, through introductions from friends, weddings, bars, clubs. It turned out that the list actually ended up like this: bars, clubs, parties, through friends, weddings.[37]

Your specific order will vary, but there are two applicable lessons there: (1) You have to try going out to all sorts of different places,

---

[34] Watch out for Roman Polanski when you're there—he's all hands.

[35] Too late. He and I have already started the wealth-transfer process. So long, suckers.

[36] Plus, if he blows you off, you'll gain a new respect for all the guys you've rejected through the years.

[37] This list, of course, excludes many other places where I found success. But I doubt 21-year-old Sam really would've believed that 31-year-old Sam would date like 15 different girls he met playing coed kickball. And if he had, he sure as hell would've signed up for coed kickball on the spot.

because *you never know what environments are going to surprise you.* And (2) once you have some experience and can draw some conclusions about where you're at your best, make sure to steer your group of friends toward those places whenever you can. Even if you just *know* they're going to say, "Really, Kevin, *another* church picnic?"

(11) You're too focused on what you're doing tomorrow. *Every night out reaches a tipping point,* usually as midnight approaches. It's the point where you can say, "I'm all in, let's have one more drink here then go to another bar and see where the night goes" . . . or "Ya know, I'm gonna cut myself off, I really want to go running in the morning, and I must—*must*—go curtain shopping tomorrow."

I'm not saying that option B is categorically bad. Some nights really just *don't* work. It's only categorically bad if you're *always* going for that option—you're not giving yourself a fair chance. When you're married you'll have plenty of time for errands, chores, and curtains. This is the era where you can shoot tequila, dance non-ironically to Sir Mix-A-Lot's greatest hits, and hop into a cab with a bunch of random people to go to a 3 AM after party.[38] At least once in a while.

---

[38]   As for curtains, all you need to worry about is taping a dark sheet over the window because you got home as the sun was coming up.

11 Good Places (That Aren't Bars or Parties) to Pick Someone Up

In reverse order, leading up to the best of the best.

(11) Grocery stores. Grocery stores are an extremely low-pressure environment to meet someone who lives in your neighborhood. But . . . if you are going to pick someone up at a grocery store, know *you'll be heavily judged on the contents of your cart;* things like bowel-moving yogurt, any meat in a can that's not tuna, store-brand gin, baby food, kid-only stuff like Cookie Crisp or purple ketchup, more than $2 worth of ramen noodles (or approximately 20 packages), store-brand sushi, a turkey baster, jugged wine, and, especially, clearance-priced, just-past-expiration meat.

(10) Rehab/AA meetings. You've taken a giant, probably life-saving step toward self-improvement—*do you really want to distract yourself* for the sake of a few go-rounds of "Wow, this used to feel a lot better high/drunk" sex? On the other hand, who better to date as you start the next phase of your life?[39]

(9) The gym. The gym is filled with people who are, in theory, in better physical shape than the average population. Just watch out for a couple of pitfalls. One, if you get rejected, you may have to see him/her day after day unless you change your entire workout schedule or switch gyms.[40]

And two, some people really *are* there to work out. So *know how to target the people who aren't.* If you're looking for a

---

[39] And that phase is: You, as a smoker. I think recovering alcoholics are the main people keeping the cigarette industry alive at this point. Oh, and you're sober. Well done, sir or ma'am.

[40] And based on the way they structure memberships, quitting a gym is tougher than the steaks you bought at clearance, just-past-expiration prices.

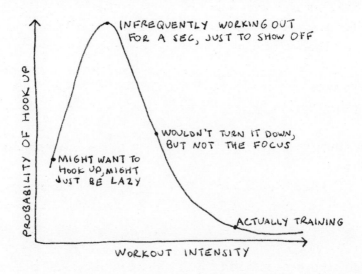

guy, pick one who's in great shape but doesn't seem to actually be concentrating on working out. He picks up a weight, lifts it a few times, walks around, takes a drink of water, talks to a meathead, repeats. He's not focusing. He probably blasted his lats and twonked his delts hours ago and now he's just there to hang out.

If you're looking for a woman, find one who's wearing makeup, and preferably wearing one of those eighties Jazzercise outfits with the turquoise thong on the outside of the spandex pants.

(8) Adult classes and workshops. Years ago, I worked in a big office building. One of the other tenants was an adult education annex that would teach all of the usual courses—How to Become a Millionaire, Strip for Your Wife, The Secrets to Turning On Your Computer, etc.

And I was perpetually shocked to see how many hundreds of people were taking those classes—and how many of them would sit together during lunch. It was like they spent three hours learning about the location of the power button on their computer *and* monitor and *all of a sudden they're lifelong friends.*

So if you sign up for a class or workshop, there's a chance you'll walk out of there with a date (*and* a whole bunch of new knowledge).[41]

(7) Work. There's nothing wrong with dating in the workplace, as long as you're smart, mature, and responsible. A lot of us spend more time with our coworkers (getting held down by The Man together) than we spend with family and friends. Yes, *it has the potential to invent new, horrifying levels of ugliness* if something goes wrong—but that's six months from now's problem, right?[42]

(6) Your friends' coworkers. Have your friends give you a heads up when they're doing happy hour with coworkers. Even if you're gun-shy about dipping your pen in your own company's ink, *this is your friend's company's ink.* It's a totally different, much more in-bounds batch of ink. (It's also a place to eat far away from where you produce excrement, if you prefer that more lowbrow euphemism.)

(5) Weddings. Everyone knows the reasons weddings are good hookup spots. I'll only caution against getting your expectations too high. I've been to plenty of weddings where there were almost no single people; since friend groups tend to get married in clusters, the number of singles can drop precipitously, and quickly. Also, for whatever reason, *the ratio of single guys to single girls never seems to match up quite right* at a wedding—and somehow, you'll always feel like you're on the wrong side of the balance.[43]

(4) Religious mixers. My parents met at a singles mixer at their synagogue. And I think that sentence alone sums up why these

---

[41] Not to mention a belly full of complimentary coffee and your pockets stuffed with Splenda packets.
[42] Check out "11 Ways to Date a Coworker (Even Your Boss) without Making a Mess" list for plenty of suggestions on how to pull this off.
[43] That's the Murphy's Law of weddings. Not to be confused with the Megan's Law of weddings, which is why you can't sit at the kids' table anymore.

are both good and bad. If you go to a singles dinner at your church or a latke fry at your synagogue or *So You Think You Can Ramadance* at your mosque, you certainly will meet lots of good prospects—to marry.

Even if you don't *think* you're going to find your future spouse, *when you meet someone at your house of worship, your relationship will fall under a different set of expectations.* Just try it out. Tell your parents, "I met someone at Mass on Easter Sunday." Compare that with the reaction from when you told them, "I met someone drinking massive margaritas during Sunday Funday."

(3) The Internet. The *opportunities to meet someone online don't end with dating sites.* Social media, Craigslist, and even old-school message boards and chat rooms can also connect two people who wouldn't have otherwise met.[44]

The only reason I put the Internet third is because, unlike the two things ranked higher, nothing can compare to meeting someone face-to-face. In two minutes of face-to-face talking, where you can read body language and facial expressions, you can pretty much figure a person out better than you could with hundreds of hours of instant messaging—even video chatting.

(2) Hard-core athletic training groups for some, coed adult sports for others. A few years into adult life, you figure out which athletic path you're taking. Are you going to train for Ironman triathlons or play softball with a beer in your hand? Either way, *when you join up with others on the same path, you're probably going to end up dating one of 'em.*

---

[44] I had an old coworker who was such a big *Lord of the Rings* fan—and such a dead ringer for Gollum—that he eventually rose to moderator level on a *LotR* message board. There, he cyber-met a woman who was also an obsessive *LotR* fan. Eventually they decided to meet . . . they got engaged . . . and he moved from L.A. to her house in rural Tennessee. I guess he did succeed in his quest to get himself the ring.

I took the coed sports path. I never would've believed this, but these coed adult sports leagues are getting more and more popular . . . and are, unequivocally, gold mines for single people. When you're playing softball, flag football, dodgeball, WAKA kickball, or curling with a bunch of other people your age—then all going out to the league's official bar afterward—it's hard *not* to meet a ton of new dating prospects.

The only way you can screw this up is by being the guy who gets too competitive. There's always one. No one wants to hook up with the guy who cursed out the referee in a coed flag football game because he was allowing bump-and-run coverage beyond five yards. (Hint: Every team has one guy who's taking things too seriously. And if you look around and don't see him . . .)

(1) Friends of your friends' boy/girlfriends. Having your friends' boy/girlfriends set you up is the best way to meet new people to date. They have entire networks of new people to hook you up with—and *they'll be happy to do it.*

The only time you should hold off on tapping this resource is if you're in "I just want to date a bunch of people, I really don't want to settle down right now" mode. Then it's a bit shortsighted and selfish to be set up with someone's friends. When you break things off after a few weeks, your friend's boy/girlfriend has to apologize to the person you just broke up with, your friend has to apologize to their new boy/girlfriend for your behavior, and the person you broke up with now eternally feels awkward around you and your friends.[45]

---

[45] Number of uses of the word "friends" in that point: 10. It's like the 2002 Emmys.

11 Awful Spots to Try to Pick Someone Up

In reverse order, ultimately leading up to the worst of the worst.

(11) Jury duty. Because our court system is hopelessly backed up, the ratio of time spent hanging around doing nothing at jury duty versus time spent doing actual jury-ing is about 15 to 1. So *you get a lot of time with your fellow jurors.* There are three reasons, though, why this is not the target-rich scenario that it seems:

(1) The only thing people want to do at jury duty is get the hell out of jury duty.[46]

(2) Ibid.[47]

(3) Secrets get revealed. When I was in a jury pool a few years ago being vetted by the attorneys, I found out everyone else's marital history, criminal history, political beliefs, and prejudices. It's too much knowledge to have before a date. I don't need to know you're divorced, you have seven DUIs, you oppose gay marriage, and you don't trust Koreans. I mean, who wants to date someone who's divorced?

(10) Sex stores. A man shopping by himself at a sex store knows he's being kinda creepy. With the amount of porn available on the Internet, if a guy's at an adult store, it's probably buying extra kinky hardware or an inanimate (possibly inflatable) object to fornicate with.

---

[46] Once someone's let go, he/she is gone—even that cute one you went to lunch with during your break yesterday. The second one of the lawyers has the judge dismiss him/her . . . gone. There are no good-byes or exchanges of contact info. Before you can say, "So do you wanna go grab—" he/she will be in the car tearing out of the lot.

[47] Ibid.

A woman also only has one of two agendas. She either wants to buy something to spice up her relationship and prove to her husband that she's not as boring in bed as he claims . . . or buy some masturbatory aid with cash, because she doesn't want her credit card linked to a vibrator on the Internet.

Either way, *neither gender wants any conversation*— they just want to get in, get out, and get the purchase home so it can take its proper place: buried under a pile of stuff in the closet.

(9) Job interviews. As you're heading into a job interview, you need to have a quick talk with your loins—*this is one of the few times you absolutely must turn your libido down to zero* and interact solely on a platonic level. Remember: It's easier to go without sex than without a home. If you go homeless, you're definitely not getting laid (except maybe by other homeless people— but probably not).

And job interviews aren't just a bad place to pick people up because they occur in an antisexual vacuum. They're bad because every single person there is dying for a reason to screw you over: your fellow candidates who want a leg up, hiring managers looking for people to do stupid things to make their cuts easier, the parking attendant who will charge you $8 if you even go 10 seconds over your validation, everyone.

(8) Your favorite restaurant. You know the one—you go there at least twice a week. You've got that one waiter or waitress today, the one who's cute and funny and even laughs at your terrible jokes.

"How's the crab roll today?"

"It's really great. People have been raving, very tender crab—"

"OK, I'll have it; you don't have to overshell it!"

"Ha!"

Pass. *If you strike out, you've just made every single trip to your favorite restaurant uncomfortable.* There's an infinite supply of potential dates out there; there's only one place within walking distance from work that serves such an incredible Chinese chicken salad for $7.99.

(7) Reality television. If you go on a reality show to find love, you will fail. Do not delude yourself into thinking that it's possible. *There's no such thing as finding love when an entire squad of TV producers are watching your every move,* trying to squeeze every ounce of drama out of you.

Someone on that show is always going to be more willing to graphically humiliate him/herself for the sake of a television camera—and there's no way those producers are going to let an elimination ceremony end where you got a rose, or necklace, or a giant Flavor Flav clock and he/she didn't.

(6) Family members' weddings. It's really hard to seduce your cousin's old sorority sisters with *your grandma looking on* and your mom continually reminding you how many drinks you've had so far.

(5) Nude beach. Approaching a stranger and trying to hit on him/her is awkward enough. Doing it fully exposed is inconceivable.[48] *Even if it's not awkward for you, it will be for the person you're hitting on.* When two naked strangers converse, greater than or equal to one of them will feel awkward. It's an irrefutable mathematical fact.[49]

Plus, I don't know what kind of spectacular body you've got, but I know that I don't like to bust mine out until I've laid on enough personality charm that my patchy chest hair or shockingly gargantuan thighs won't be a deal breaker.

---

[48] Even more inconceivable than winning a fencing match, outwrestling a giant, AND developing an immunity to certain types of poison.

[49] Kind of like Sex with Psycho Person + Condom = Pregnancy.

(4) An obscure dating website. There are only a few reasons someone would eschew the Match.coms and eHarmony.coms of the world and sign up for some site like online-dating-today.net:

(1) He/she has been flagged on a big dating site for a failed background check; (2) He's married and figures his wife won't search for him on a smaller site; (3) She's a Soviet mail-order bride or, worse, part of a pyramid scheme looking for people to sell knife sets to;[50] (4) He/she is the kind of person who is susceptible to clicking links in spam e-mails, which is a sign that he/she has many deal-breaking flaws just under the surface.

Stick to the big sites, where they've invested millions of dollars and have full-time employees eradicating shady characters. I know this feels like the online equivalent of shopping at Home Depot instead of supporting your local mom-and-pop store—but in this case, you really are better off feeding the giant empire.

(3) Movies with certain touchy themes. Some movies are turn-ons, and most of the rest are neutral. A few, though, *are pretty much guarantees that you'll leave the theater without a new number* in your phone.

I'd avoid movies about any cancer, movies about parents and children who are separated and eventually reunited, and movies where Jews are killed and/or oppressed. Cancer movies are *way* too depressing and hit too close to home for everyone; parent/child movies make you sentimental and want to listen to John Denver, not hit on someone; and movies about the Jewish struggle are always made so extravagantly and brilliantly[51] that they make you just want to go out and hug your banker.

---

[50] Far more on using dates to move pyramid scheme products is coming your way in the "11 Ideas for Dates That Will Backfire Brutally" list.

[51] Some would say that's because my fellow Jews run the entertainment industry; I say stop

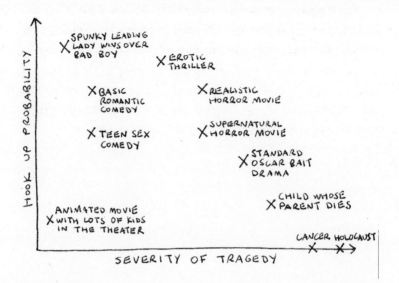

(2) Bachelorette parties of four women or fewer. A small bachelorette party means that *every girl plays an indispensable role.*

The bride gets too drunk[52] . . . the maid-of-honor stays sober to make sure the bride is OK . . . another girl has a boyfriend or husband . . . and that leaves the one single girl who feels too guilty breaking off from the tiny group to talk to a guy.

So just don't bother. If you're a guy, you only have a shot with girl number four, and after you talk to her for three minutes the rest of the group is going to drag her away. And if you're that girl, just recognize that this weekend isn't going to lead to anything exciting for you, other than acquiring yet another penis straw. (Not a euphemism.)

---

being so cynical, or I'll ruin your credit rating.

[52]   Either because she's sad she doesn't have a lot of friends, or because she subconsciously doubts the fun-making ability of the tiny group and decides 15 Malibu shots is the only way to liven up the night.

(1) Rallies for causes you're only kinda into. Go support a charity or cause you're really into. Hit the site of an oil spill and scrape plants and rocks and pelicans. But if you're mostly going for dating purposes, *you're not going to find the endless sea of young, cool, progressive, available options you'd like.* No one who's truly dedicated to a cause likes a carpetbagger. And now, even worse, you're stuck doing *charity work.* Ouch.

11 Secrets for Dating When You're Self-Conscious about Your Weight

In my early 20s, when I was one bad sunburn away from looking like the Kool-Aid Man, I got a ton of first-hand experience on what it's like to date when you're self-conscious about your weight. I learned many, many lessons about what didn't work. And like three about what did.[53]

(1) Sacrifice one month to tone up your body . . . and confidence. Saying, "I'm overweight, no one's going to date me," is a cop-out. Your size may play into the equation but your confidence carries much more . . . ahem . . . weight.

You can't fake confidence. You can *almost* fake it. You can hold your chin up and put a smirk on your face and respond to a question like, "What's your name?" with "I don't know if you deserve to find out." But your true confidence level will still leak out in everything you say and do.

The good news: You can legitimately increase your confidence in one month. You just have to devote yourself, hardcore, to one month of serious diet and exercise. All those horribly unpleasant things: reduce calories, carbs, and sugar; cut *way* down on drinking; and aim to hit the gym daily. Thirty days for the rest of your life.[54] When

---

[53] Fact: Being funny did not. I've been making a living doing comedy writing since age 23, but women just failed to notice my sense of humor until I lost a lot of weight. Since all women say that a great sense of humor is the most important quality in a guy, it must just be a coincidence.

[54] Maybe I'm co-opting James van der Beek's speech at the climax of *Varsity Blues* there, and maybe I'm not.

the month is over, you will see—and *feel*—a change in your body. And your confidence.

(2) Identify the good and bad places to meet people. There are two key places: (1) at friends' parties where you have an "in"; and (2) through online dating. In both cases, you can feel more confident because your personality can do some of the heavy lifting . . . *rather than having to deal on an exclusively superficial level* with random strangers at a bar.

(3) Be honest with your online dating photos. Everyone knows the tricks: photos shot above your head at a downward angle can strip off dozens and dozens of pounds, *photos from when you had mono* (sure, you look like you've been on an island hanging out with a volleyball . . . but damn, so slim), photos from a petting zoo where a friendly alpaca is strategically blocking your trouble areas.

To have real success—like multiple dates—you have to be honest. After your one month of diet and exercise is up, put on some black clothes and take a few full-body shots.

(4) Set your goals just slightly higher than you think you should. When you're feeling self-conscious about your appearance, you'll feel an instinct to weed out potential people because they're out of your league. At least you think they are. You're your own harshest critic.[55]

While *only* targeting the gold medals like astronauts and supermodels and nerd-hip bloggers-cum-authors will probably leave you rejected, *eliminating them unilaterally will make you feel like you've entered settling mode.* Which really isn't necessary.

---

[55] Unless you're Italian, Jewish, WASPy, or Indian, in which case the females over 50 in your family are your harshest critics. If you're Asian, the males over 50 join in, too.

(5) Eliminate clothes and grooming choices that make you look heavier. I always enjoy watching *The Biggest Loser*[56] and, every season, after a few months of unnaturally extreme weight loss, the show gives the contestants makeovers. I find it stunning; there are men who've lost 120, 140 pounds . . . but when the stylists cut their long, raggedy hair, *then* they finally look skinny.

There are things you can do to slim yourself and things you can do to make yourself look heavier. For men, things like long shaggy hair, bad facial hair, and baggy clothing are awful. For women, not everyone can wear everything—and dressing to flatter your body is more important than dressing ultra-trendy.

(6) If you want to mention your weight on a date, do it once in a funny way and move on. When I was doing stand-up comedy, we talked about a concept called the "elephant in the room." If you're onstage and suddenly an elephant barged into a comedy club (most likely to try the veal and not tip his waitress), in order to maintain an honest relationship with the audience, you need to stop your routine and comment on the elephant.

Although I hate to use an elephant-based analogy for this, you may have the same instinct when you're on a date. You feel a little uneasy about your weight or you think he/she's uneasy about your weight, so *if you make a joke about it you'll both be more comfortable.*

I personally chose to never talk about my body insecurities on a first date because I was kinda hoping she hadn't noticed.[57] But if you do feel the need to say something, make one good joke . . . and move

---

[56] Motto: "NBC asked us to fill two freaking prime time hours a week, so be prepared to watch a LOT of footage of 380-pound people on treadmills." Secondary motto: "Never, ever watch this without at least a 45-minute DVR buffer."

[57] Obviously, she had. But I'd always try to convince myself she hadn't. These little mental tricks kept me going.

on. Dwelling shows insecurity, draws focus to your size, and will end up making your date *less* comfortable, not more.

(7) Eat "normal" on a date. If you just order a side salad, your weight becomes the unspoken subtext of the entire date. That also happens if you go the other way and order a giant bowl of fettuccini Alfredo with an entire loaf of bread. (If you do happen to be running a marathon the next day, then that carbo-loading is fine—or if you're bulking up to play the role of Bridget Jones.)

By ordering a regular-sized meal, maybe subbing out a fried side dish for vegetables, and splitting a dessert, *your food issues don't have to become the date's food issues.*

(8) Maintain full confidence when it's time to hook up. Two things to remember once things start to get physical: (1) *Pull off those clothes without shame*, and (2) once someone's gotten to that point with you, his/her libido has taken over the reins, and reaching down and touching a little extra love around your belly isn't *close* to a strong enough force to stop this Iditarod.

(9) Go on the Dating Diet. After you've done your month of dieting and exercising, chances are you'll want to keep going. But you *need to start cashing in on your slimness-induced confidence, too.* I came up with the Dating Diet for that occasion.

Eat extremely healthy, and cut out alcohol completely, except when you're on a date. You won't lose weight as fast as you would if you, say, only ate sprouts and paste for a month. . . . but you'll keep gradually losing weight in a very, very mentally healthy way.

(10) Don't blame everything that goes wrong on your weight. So you went out on a date, things seemed to go really well . . . and then you never heard from the person again. You know the first thing that pops into your head.

The number on the scale is not *the* definitive reason every time a date goes wrong—and it's a lazy excuse. Rather than examining what didn't go right on the date—why the connection you felt wasn't reciprocated, or why this keeps happening—you're blaming a bias that you assume other people have.[58] *By blaming dating failures only on weight, you limit your growth.*

(11) Don't think there's something wrong with people for dating you. This is a weird confidence transference thing. When someone goes on a date with you, and seems to like you, and wants to go out again, *there's not something wrong with him/her.*

You're not dealing with a chubby chaser, someone who's just using you, or someone who has some major flaw that keeps him/her un-dateable by the general populous. He/she just isn't as hung up on your weight as you are, so fight your urge to be less interested because he/she's more interested. There are people out there who will love you even though you're carrying some extra weight. For reference, watch any CBS sitcom.

---

[58]   It reminds me of this friend from college who used to blame every misfortune, no matter how minor, on people's discrimination against him because he's Asian. Bad grades, rejection from women, bad service at restaurants, his bad driving—everything.

11 Best and Worst
Coed Drinking Games

We're in an era where drinking games no longer have to be lumped in with things like bunk beds, mini fridges, black-light posters, and shower sandals—all left behind in college. I know this thanks to Facebook. Rather than having to *talk* to long-lost summer camp and elementary school friends and ask each of them, "Are you still as immature as I am?" I just pull up their pages. Everyone's holding one of two things: a baby . . . or a red plastic cup.

The ever-enduring popularity of drinking games is good when you're single, because games are exceptionally social activities and, in the right context, perfect ways to meet new people.

Here are the 11 best and worst coed drinking games—some of which are terribly counterproductive to your dating and hooking up life; some of which will make it go way, way better. That's right: Drinking is by *far* the lower priority.

(1) GOOD: Flip cup. The entire time I was in school (through 2001), I never once played flip cup. It just wasn't a big game then. Now, a decade later, it's king of the drinking game world.[59] (Totally a phenomenon born in the 2000s, like mixed martial arts, *American*

---

[59] The reasons for flip cup's ascension make perfect sense. There's no physical advantage for men or women. The amount of drinking per round is easy, so even the girls who say, "Oh my gosh, I just hate beer" can handle it. You can play as teams or solo. The game is so simple that it doesn't get bogged down in all the "MY school did it this way . . ." rules that plague beer pong and others. And, most important, for what it is, it's disproportionately entertaining.

Idol, and buying a home using only the two quarters and lint in your pocket as a down payment.)

Hop in on a game at a party. *Position yourself across the table from someone you want to talk to, and start a faux-rivalry.* Some playful trash talking, guarantees of victory, that kind of stuff. As the game winds down or teams get reshuffled, make the very easy transition into having a real conversation with your "rival."

(2) BAD: Asshole. It's just not a unifying experience. It engenders resentment, always breaks down into an anarchist mess, and discourages friendly banter between you and strangers. Also, Jane Austen would roll over in her grave if she knew you were trying to court someone by saying, *"Give me all your twos, then drink, asshole."*

(3) GOOD: "I Never"/"Never Have I Ever." Three positives here: (1) Hinting at all the deviant stuff you've done makes you all tighter; (2) it's great if you want to play a game at a bar but don't have dice or cards and don't want to start trying to flip glass pints; and (3) it's a spectacular way to *identify whether someone's sexual freakiness and alcohol/drug use level matches up with yours.*

(4) TRICKY BUT GOOD: Beer pong/Beirut. Beer pong can be a blast. *It can also be a game where men alienate women by becoming too competitive*—believe it or not, "really aggressive during beer pong" has yet to be found on a single woman's "qualities I look for in a guy" list. Here are two ways to use *coed* beer pong to your advantage.

(1) *Two coed teams of two.* You and your partner are isolated for some quality one-on-one time at a party *and* get to develop that bunker mentality as teammates. Or, (2) try *two guys against two girls.* You'll want to play more than one game—stay together on the

table for a while—and, eventually, propose a friendly wager on a game.[60]

(5) GOOD: King's cup. Every person who's ever played this game has his/her own set of rules. (And not in a cool, James Dean way of playing by your own rules—more like "Oh, you play that eights mean all the guys take a drink? Weird.")[61]

It's good because *you can include a lot of people,* it doesn't take any motor skill so it's not prohibitive to rookies, and it gives you a chance to show off your sense of humor and personality.

(6) BAD: Caps.[62] In my experience with caps, men love it, women hate it. It's like Scarlett Johansson.

As fun as caps is with your buddies, *it's the most antisocial, exclusionary game ever,* meant only to be played by four male friends when no women are within 500 yards. (I didn't even pick that number arbitrarily. I could legitimately see women going to a judge to get a restraining order against caps.)

---

[60] Several years back, my friend Noah and I found ourselves in this scenario and ended up betting these girls we were playing that the losers had to do a pole dance for the winners, with the winners being the poles. We thought we were brilliant. Then we somehow lost the game and the potentially sexy situation turned into a tragicomedy of unparalleled levels. Apparently my stripper pole moves are way more funny than seductive. So . . . um . . . if you use that bet idea, make sure the girls lose.

[61] At least the basic fundamentals are the same. You lay out a deck of cards facedown around a cup, go in a circle taking turns selecting a card, and each different card has an activity associated with it. Beyond that, this thing has more regional differences than the name people call sub sandwiches.

[62] Not everyone knows caps, and it's definitely not as universal as the rest of the games on this list. Basically, it involves two teams of two, sitting on the floor 10–12 feet away from each other, trying to throw bottle caps into the other team's cup. It sounds stupid. My close friends and I may or may not play in the national tournament of this game every year, where, in our early 30s, we're among the youngest competitors. In fact, one of the lists in this book was written in a hotel room in San Diego while we were down there for the 2010 caps tourney. Try to guess which one.

(7) BAD: Chugging contest. It's really *lose-lose as a coed activity.* If someone tries but fails to, say, chug three beers in four minutes,[63] that person just feels sick. And if someone succeeds, watching him or (yes) her pound down drinks—and then wipe a little spillage off the sides of his/her face, neck, and shirt collar all while burping—is hard to spin as a turn-on.

(8) GOOD: Thumper. When I was in sixth grade, my teacher would occasionally have us play Thumper when the class was getting bored and zoning out. Several years later, I found out Thumper is a great drinking game, for the exact same reason.[64]

Bust out Thumper when you're in a group and people are dragging. You can include an unlimited number of people, nondrinkers can play, too, and it raises the group's energy level by getting everyone moving around and laughing.

(9) BAD: Grenade.[65] There's *nothing good about having a shaken-up beer explode in your face.* And don't try to mine a sexual metaphor out of that. Trust me, when you play, it ain't sexy.

(10) BAD: Watch a movie/TV show and drink when certain things happen. This almost *always* works better in theory than in practice. The energy gets sucked out of the room—everyone's just kind of sitting there, watching TV. The drinking happens at a bad pace, generally not fast enough to lead to any intoxication, but

---

[63] My friend Adam actually created a "game" based around this idea. He called it Trois Bier. You put a song on and everyone tries to finish three beers during the course of the song. It's gross.

[64] I wonder what I would've thought if, in sixth grade, a gypsy fortune teller would've told me that Thumper and kickball would majorly factor into my late 20s. Actually, at that point I probably would've just looked at her and said, "Don't have a cow, man."

[65] Grenade is a game that I learned about from Europeans; apparently it's big over there. You put a bunch of beer cans in a bag and shake the HELL out of one. Shake it to the point where Andre 3000 is like, "Whoa, child, slow it down." Then everyone stands in a circle and, one-by-one, each person draws a beer out of the bag and opens them right underneath his or her nose. If it wasn't shaken up, the person drinks it. If it was shaken up, well, you can imagine. This game never makes it past one round.

just fast enough that, after the movie or show's over, everyone's in that in-between zone of "I guess we could drink more, but are we *really* gonna rally and go out now?"

And, worst of all, *no one is talking to anyone else because you're too busy paying attention for drinking clues.* Sure, it's funny (and puts you in danger of alcohol poisoning) to take a drink every time a guy starts crying on *The Bachelorette* or Uncle Joey does an impression of Popeye on Full House. But it's not going to lead to anything beyond that.

(11) BAD: Shot contest. Slamming a bottle of bourbon down on the table and going shot-for-shot against someone until one person passes out crosses the line from *"good ol' fashioned Kentucky schoolyard game"* to *"time for an intervention."* When you send a person into a spiral of reevaluating all of their life choices, it's damn near impossible to follow it up with, "So you wanna go out sometime?"

2

Communication

To say I was just not into the movie version of *He's Just Not That into You* would just not be a strong enough way for me to convey to you just how not into that movie I was.

I don't know how it compares to the book—I mean, who reads dating books anymore, right?—but I know I couldn't handle the movie because it completely betrayed its underlying thesis. And if there's one thing I don't stand for, it's schlock movies betraying their underlying theses.[66]

The grandiose principle of the movie (and I assume book)—and the one that made its creators 14 garbage trucks full of money—is that you're the rule, not the exception. When you date a guy, the odds are overwhelmingly against you two living happily ever after (or even happily going on a second date). He's not that into you, and there's nothing you can do to change that. One day you *will* meet the guy who *is* into you, and then you'll get to sail off to Fairytale Island where it only rains long enough to make rainbows, and you are beautiful in every single way, so words can't bring you down.

---

[66] Martin Luther did *not* stay up all night with his hammer and nail for *that*.

Naturally, the movie ends by crapping on that thesis completely. Pretty much all of the women actually being the exceptions, with all the guys being just that into them. It's the *Wayne's World* mega-happy ending.

In the movie, Drew Barrymore delivers a monologue about dating in this era, and it goes, "I had this guy leave me a voice mail at work, so I called him at home, and then he e-mailed me to my BlackBerry, and so I texted to his cell, and now you just have to go around checking all these different portals just to get rejected by seven different technologies. It's exhausting."[67]

And I just couldn't disagree with her more. Technology, when used properly, shouldn't make your dating life more difficult . . . it should make things easier than ever.

This chapter is all about the way we communicate when we're dating. When every text message, every delayed return phone call, and every Facebook status update is analyzed. When you get a message to your phone and hold it up to your friends and say "Now what does *this* mean?" And where you try to use every piece of technology at your disposal to make your dating life blow up (in the rapper-getting-famous way) and not blow up (in the building-being-demolished-due-to-infestation way).

. So whether you're a high school senior on your parents' computer trying to Skype your way to My First Booty Call; a woman in your mid-20s who can't figure out why you're getting two dates, then never hearing from guys again; a guy in your mid-30s who just got a number, now trying to figure out how long to wait before you text her; or a new divorcée in your mid-50s staring at Twitter and wondering why in the hell it exists—it's time to decode the messages, send the right signals, and communicate like a pro.

---

[67] I guess she's come a long way from the days where she was getting rejected by aliens who just wanted to phone home.

Otherwise, you're going to be like Drew Barrymore, wondering why a guy isn't gChatting your iPhone when his Friendster says he's Foursquaring right down the street—and I promise, you're just not that into that.

11 Secret Meanings behind
Punctuation in Text Messages

The way you use an exclamation point can change your dating life.

Texting removes the vocal cues we once used to overanalyze if someone liked us. Now we have to look at 140 to 160 characters—and with less raw data to work with, our overanalyzing hits a whole different level of insanity. One key aspect of that insanity is reading way too much into every nuance of every text message, especially punctuation. So . . . here are the clues his/her punctuation choices are sending (and also the clues you're sending right back).

(1) Period.

Meaning: You don't want to keep going back and forth all night.

In texting, you don't have to end a sentence with any punctuation. It's totally acceptable to just let it dangle. So using a period gives a certain air of finality to a statement. Compare:

I'm heading out to the party now.
I'm heading out to the party now

In the first one, the meaning is clear: we've had our back-and-forth over text, but I have plans, and they do not include continuing this conversation—period. In the second one, **without the period, it feels much more open-ended**—I'm heading out to the party *now* but who knows what I'm doing later, and you just might be part of it. Periods end things.[68] Leaving one out keeps things open.

---

[68] Including pregnancy scares. Am I right? Ladies!?

(2) Exclamation point!

Meaning: Something between playful and desperate, depending on usage.

The exclamation point is the most valuable punctuation mark you have in your arsenal, but it's also the most dangerous. When used properly, a single exclamation point can set a light tone, convey excitement, and even demonstrate interest. Compare:

Sounds good. Not sure if we're going but I might see you at the party. If you leave, let me know

Sounds good. Not sure if we're going but I might see you at the party. If you leave, let me know!

The person in the second example seems far, far more interested in getting together . . . and ***did it without changing a word.***

But be careful. Exclamation points are the most abused piece of punctuation in our world today. When you start overusing exclamation points, you look like an amateur:

Sounds good! Not sure if we're going but I might see you at the party! If you leave, let me know!

The first exclamation point is OK . . . the second is way too over-eager . . . and the third is just flat-out desperate. And when in doubt, get rid of the exclamation point. It's always better to play it cool than to play it like a 12-year-old writing YouTube comments.

(3) Semicolon.

Meaning: You're trying too hard.

No one uses semicolons in day-to-day casual writing; it's a literary piece of punctuation, not a colloquial one. So using a semicolon in a text shows you've thought out, revised, and overedited your message. That means you're trying too hard, and there's nothing worse than trying too hard. ***A semicolon in a text message is the equivalent of putting on makeup to go to the gym.***

(4) Apostrophe.

Meaning: You pay attention to the little things.

In text land, apostrophes have become endangered species. Youd is just as acceptable at you'd. Id is just as acceptable as I'd. Youre is just as acceptable as you're. (Or, on the Internet, your.[69])

So when you actually take the time to use an apostrophe, it means something. I like to think *it sends a subconscious message that you take the extra time to do things right.* And that effort hints that you'd be a real hard-working giver in a relationship—or at least in one extremely memorable sexual escapade.

(5) Left and right braces.

Meaning: You're approaching this too logically.

In my experience, no one uses the left and right braces unless they're a math guy or computer programmer. Either way, they're *looking at the current romantic situation very, very logically.* Warning: Computer programming joke ahead.[70]

```
if (texts == playful) {
ask("Do you want to grab a drink sometime?")
}
else if (texts < hostile) {
date_prospects['current'] = "questionable";
date_prospects['future'] = "still possible, wait
and see";
}
else {
die();
}
```

---

[69] It's taking everything in my being to keep from launching into an its/it's rant here.

[70] I don't know why I try to do computer-programming jokes. The normals don't even read them because they assume they're prohibitively esoteric, and the programmers just point out the issues with my coding style.

(6) Asterisk.

Meaning: You're afraid the person isn't as cool as you.

The main reason people use asterisks in a text is to censor a word, for example: *"I like deep-fried sandwiches so my friends call me the C*** of Monte Cristo. Little do they know I'm plotting my elaborate revenge on them."*

And there's really only one reason to censor a swear word: *if you're afraid the person's not as cool as you.* Because if they were, they'd run around dropping f-bombs and c-bombs and f'd-in-the-a-with-your-own-d-bombs[71] without the censorship.

So asterisks imply that you don't think that person likes it raw, like you (and ODB). Save the asterisks for funny usage, something like this: *"I bet you $65,000* that I am a better bowler than you.*

*prize may be substituted for firm handshake or one turn at claw game."

(7) Plus sign.

Meaning: You've got it bad.

If you use the plus sign in lieu of the word "and" or an ampersand, it's your subconscious telling you that you *really* like the person. When couples carve their names into trees, they use a plus sign between them. "Laura + Mike. July 1991. I do it for you"; "Joe + Susan. January 1998. Our hearts will go on"; "Logan + Madison. August 2010. California gurls."

A plus sign doesn't simply translate to "and" . . . *it's a symbolic unification.* So if you send the text *"Me + you should go to Medi-*

---

[71] This is actually a quote from the first porn movie I ever saw. I don't remember the title. A woman with small breasts but jaw-droppingly long nipples said that to the guy. He responded, "That's your problem, Rosie. You don't know man's limitations." Yes, I can still quote it. I watched that movie so many times that the tape eventually wore out.

eval Times," you're really carving those Medieval Times plans—and the love therein—into a tree.[72]

(8) Emoticons.

Meaning: You want to bring the conversation to life.

Texting is a faceless, emotionless means of communication. So no matter how middle school-ish they are, emoticons can be the best way to make your texts feel 3-D (and not crappy, retrofitted 3-D like they're using in movies to add to the ticket prices.[73] Good 3-D).

For women, use them carefully. *Too many and you look immature.* I had a friend who was texting with a girl and every single message she sent contained the winky face. It's like she was outsourcing her texting to a seventh grader. (Or that her emoticon had some kind of palsy.)

And if you're male . . . steer very clear. Any ratio higher than one emoticon per one hundred texts is pure poison.

(9) Ellipses.

Meaning: You want the person to read between the lines.

Using ellipses in a text is *your way of saying what you either can't say yet* (because it'd fall under the "too soon" umbrella), or what you are afraid to say (because you're afraid you'll seem disagreeable or high maintenance). Check out this example:

Yeah, Kickboxer 4 *could work . . . I've also heard good things about that Katherine Heigl movie* Falling in Love Is Neat . . . *either way, meet you there at 8?*

---

[72] And that kind of eco-vandalism might sit OK with the Green Knight—because, if I recall correctly, both times I've been to Medieval Times they've made him the dickhead one—but no one else.

[73] I'm fairly sure this will prove to be the most dated reference I make in this book. Although I did mention Foursquare, and that thing will probably die between the time I finish the manuscript and the book goes to press.

It's clear what that text really means: "I'd rather die than see a movie about the underground world of kickboxing, and you're an idiot for suggesting that we go see it. I'd rather see a romantic comedy. And now, because this has gotten a little awkward, I think we should meet at the theater so I have an escape plan."

You can also use ellipses in a positive way, to get the person's imagination going:

Had maybe a few too many drinks last night . . . legs are sore from dancing . . . in the bathtub right now . . .

That text takes three statements and just loads them with sexual undertones thanks to the ellipses. (Unless a guy sent that text. Then it's just kind of odd.)

(10) Question marks.

Meaning: It depends on how many question marks you use.

Question marks have a tendency to stack onto each other. And *with each stack the meaning changes.*

What time do you want to meet up? Simple, unassuming, and friendly. Gets the point across, elicits a response, but also drives toward a solution.

What time do you want to meet up?? Looks like a typo.

What time do you want to meet up??? Feels impatient, childish. It's an aggressive question: It demands a response, and suggests that the response had better be to your liking.

What time do you want to meet up???? Cycles back to playful. Now it's a joke. If you (God forbid) talked to the person on the phone, you might sing-say that entire question.

What time do you want to meet up????? Too many. Now it's just confusing. Why were five question marks necessary? This seems like the kind of person who would write "kewl."

So . . . use one question mark to just move the conversation along, and four to move it along flirtatiously. Anything else and you're doing it wrong.[74]

(11) Tilde.

Meaning: You're either a punctuation master not confined to the traditional system . . . or you're Hispanic.

Either way, *you sound like a catch to me.*

---

[74] I did think about going all the way up to 11 question marks. But I have a max number of words I'm allowed to use in this book, and I think once you get past five question marks the message remains the same. Although, at 11, it might look like you haven't quite mastered the art of the touch screen yet.

11 Signs a Guy's Really Into You

Many of my female friends seem to encounter the same problem. They go out with a good guy, have a great time, he's nice, he's charming, lots of laughs, there's physical chemistry—and then they never hear from him again. The reason? None of those is a real sign. These are.

(1) He breaks the dating rules. As guys, we *very* quickly learn what dating moves yield us the best results. We learn where to go for dates, how long to wait before we call and text, what to say in those calls and texts, how to balance being nice with being an a-hole, and, yes, how to play with your mind so you become irrationally crazy for us.

All of those fundamentals fly out the window when we really like you. We overcommunicate. We share our feelings way too early. We seem nervous around you. We're tentative in bed. We forget everything we've ever learned about how to keep the power in a relationship, and hand you complete ownership of us.

Those fundamentals only vanish when we're not playing around, when something separates you from all the other women we're dating or have dated. It's like a baseball player who has an MVP-worthy regular season, then bats .072 in the World Series.[75] We're just overmatched by the potential and the magnitude of the situation.

---

[75] For example, anyone who's ever played on the Cleveland Indians. Man, do I love them and hate them at the same time. If the Cleveland Indians were a woman I'd totally break all the rules for her.

(2) He hates hearing about your dirtier sexual adventures. When the conversation gets sexual, share a raunchy detail of your past. It doesn't have to be over the top (". . . so I said, 'No, Joey Fatone, you don't have to leave, I have plenty of orifices to go around!'"). Just a quick confession will do. Then watch his reaction.

If he's trying to play it cool but is clearly seething, *it's because he really likes you and can't even comprehend that some unworthy jackass got to do something so deviant with his pure, sweet angel.*

If he's intrigued, stimulated, excited, or genuinely impressed, he's primarily into you for sex, and now he's embiggened[76] because you clearly have a freak side he's going to get to tap into.

(3) He has no problem with you getting *too* drunk. If he's determined to have sex with you ASAP, he won't let you get too drunk—just drunk enough that having him writhe around on top of you seems like a good idea. But if he's not trying to stop you from drinking like a Russian mule on payday, it's because he doesn't mind taking care of you later when you're throwing up in the toilet. And *there's no love like hair-holding,* back-rubbing, garbage-can-next-to-the-bed-putting love.

(4) He calls at either 1 PM or 1 AM, just to talk. No one has time for random girls at 1 p.m. That's when you just got back from lunch and have to actually work because you slacked off all morning surfing the web.[77] So if he calls or texts you then, it's because *you've fought your way to the front of his mind.*

Everyone has time for random girls at 1 AM. But not to chat about how the night went and about how much fun it was as a child to spend summers up at the lake.

---

[76] It's a perfectly cromulent word.

[77] I recommend a website called 11Points.com. I keep the cursing to an absolute minimum, so most corporate filters and firewalls haven't banned it yet.

(5) He moves really slowly sexually. On my second date with my (now) girlfriend, we kissed for the first time. And for the next three dates, again, all we did was kiss. There were two reasons. One, I knew I liked her so much that I was petrified about trying to move faster and screwing anything up. And two, since I saw so much long-term potential, I wasn't in any particular hurry.

Of course, she hadn't read this book yet (once again, I find myself screwed over by technology's failure to produce time machines[78]) so she interpreted our five dates of kissing in a completely different way: He doesn't find me at all sexually attractive, and we have no chemistry.

I want to make sure other women don't make that same erroneous assumption—that theory of hers actually came dangerously close to cutting off our fledgling relationship. So, please, internalize this: *If a guy is moving really slow with you but keeps asking you out, it's because he really likes you.* If he doesn't see much potential in the relationship, he'll try to get as far as he can as quickly as he can.[79]

(6) He talks about long-term plans . . . then brings them up again. Anyone can make long-term plans. "I've heard Belgium is beautiful this time of year." "*We* should go to Belgium!" "Absolutely. We 100 percent should."

But when a week later he's actually looking up prices on Brussels Airlines and explaining the finer points of Walloon-Flemish interaction, he's showing that *he sees you two being together for a long, long time.*

---

[78]   And you know who I blame for that? The DeLorean Motor Company for going belly-up. If they'd just stuck it out I'd have a Sports Almanac in my greedy little hands right now and a hoverboard under my feet.

[79]   Now, this isn't to say that a guy would refuse to have sex with you early on if it happened to fall into his lap (that's semifigurative, semiliteral, by the way). But slowness is unmistakable. Stop worrying—if he keeps asking you out, it's a guarantee that he's sexually attracted to you.

To put it another way, if he's looking up flights to Belgium, he's not waffling about his feelings toward you.

(7) He tries to reach common ground with your friends. If I'm dating a girl and feeling kinda whatever about it, I don't care how her friends feel about me. I know I'm never going to see them again in a month, and *they're going to talk shit about me anyway.*[80]

But if I want to be around for the long **haul**, it's important for me to sow some **oats**.[81] I know I'm going to see these people a lot, so I'm going to put everything I've got into making sure they like me—and making sure that I like them, too.

(8) He finds little random ways to see you. His water isn't working, and he needs to come take a shower? He's got a meeting tomorrow right around the corner? Of all the gym joints in all the towns in all the world he walks into yours? *These things don't happen by accident.* If it walks like a duck and quacks like a duck and seems to be borderline stalking another duck . . .

(9) He has no problem including you in plans with his friends. My girlfriend once told me a story about the guy she was dating before me. She was just coming back from a week away and called to see if he could get her from the airport. "Ooh, I can't," he told her, "my friends and I are going to be at a bar watching football." Not only did he veto the airport pickup, he let that sentence linger and die there, as she waited for a "you should come meet us" that never arrived.

I bring this up for two reasons: (1) To remind her how good she has it; and (2) because it leads to a much grander point: *Guys know*

---

[80] "You're better off without him. You didn't want your kids to end up with that nose. Seriously, when he turned sideways I think he caused an eclipse. And not a good eclipse, like *The Twilight Saga: Eclipse. Such* a bounce back after that *New Moon* disaster."

[81] That is, without a doubt, my favorite line of this book.

the right things to do. We really do. We intentionally choose not to do them when we want to keep our distance. So when a guy *does* invite you out, it means he's choosing to make the right moves—the moves he believes will really win you over.

(10) His friends are in serious relationships, and it's been a little while since he was in one. No, this isn't 100 percent connected to *you*. You're a cool girl who happened to be at the right place at the right time. I know that's a horribly condescending and dismissive way to put it but, usually, a guy's going to get serious when he's ready to be into *someone*. And if all his friends coupled up and/or got married, and he's been dating around for a while . . . he's ready.

Marriages seem to happen in packs.[82] And *it's just as hard to be the last single friend as it was to be the first married friend.*

(11) It's how he acts when you're *not* together. This is the big one. You're dating a guy. When you're out together or talking, he very well may be the nicest, funniest, most caring, amazing guy ever; you have a blast together; he's attentive; he's perfect. But when it comes down to it a few weeks or even months later, he says he's not ready to be exclusive. And shortly after that he ends things. You just don't understand how someone who seemed so into you would do that.

The problem is that you're only judging the relationship by the time you're spending together. *The secret to figuring out what a guy's thinking is what he does during the time you're apart.*

---

[82] Just like celebrity deaths, which always seem to happen in threes, right? Even though people now just try to prove that rule: "Farrah Fawcett died, then Michael Jackson, and now Argentina's undersecretary of the treasury died, too? Man, these celebrity deaths always happen in threes." But marriage is great. It's totally not like a low-level South American bureaucrat dying a slow death.

And those are the other 10 things on this list. Does he text you to say good night and not just to try to get you to come over late? When he tells you about going to watch football with his friends, does he invite you along? When his plane lands on vacation does he let you know right away that he landed? If he's not doing those things . . . to paraphrase the title of that other book, he's just not that into the idea of possibly having a long-term potential relationship in the near- or short-term future with you.

Behavior when you're together just doesn't paint the whole picture. No one wants to have a bad time on a date. If a guy's only 50 percent into you, he's not only going to give 50 percent effort on a date—he's going to give more so he has a fun night that might end with some hand-based exploration. And then when he leaves, while you're swimming in Candy Cane Lagoon on Fairytale Island from the glorious date, he's on the way home calling or texting some other girl.

But if he's calling or texting *you* on the way home from that date, you've got him. So dig in those claws and get yourself a drawer in his dresser.

11 Signs a Girl's Really
Into You

Like the "11 Signs a Guy's Really Into You" list, the first 10 items here all build to the one ultimate, irrefutable 11th item. But don't skip ahead. Be like Usher. Take it nice and slow.[83]

(1) She makes some comment like "Finally!" after you kiss her. Women are used to guys pawing all over them; to guys totally misreading signals—or just blatantly ignoring negative ones—and plunging in, tongue first. So when, finally, she really wants someone to kiss her, and he delays it, *it vexes the hell out of her*—to the point of taking up a permanent spot in her head the entire time you're together and *not* kissing.

(2) She tries to take on your hobbies. Freshman year of college, there was a girl in my dorm who would watch pro wrestling with me every Monday night. (In my defense, it was just as the WWF-WCW Monday Night Wars were really starting to heat up.) At age 18, I suspected she had a crush on me but had no idea how to read signs. Looking back now, I can guarantee it. She watched wrestling with me every Monday night for four months. No girl should be able to tell you the name of Bret "Hitman" Hart's finishing move.[84]

Taking on your hobby makes perfect sense, of course. It means a lot to you, you spend time doing it—so, in the future, you're going to want to be with a woman who enjoys it. *She's aggressively*

---

[83] Or, if that reference isn't doing it for you, then flip it around and use a Paula Abdul "Rush, Rush" one.

[84] +15 points to anyone who just said, out loud, "Sharpshooter!" (Or anyone who went older school and said "Piledriver!" or "Hart Attack Clothesline!")

positioning herself as that woman and staking out her territory.
Other women, beware. (Koko B. Ware, that is.)

**(3) She compliments things that may not be real but are
things she wants to be real.** No matter how cool I'm trying to
make myself come off in this book, I'm well aware that I have an
endless supply of flaws. One of the big ones is my thoughtfulness.
I'm obsessed with my work—and this leads to me being completely
selfish with my time.

So I always found it funny when I'd start dating someone and
she'd tell me how thoughtful I am. Just wait until the day I decide not
to go to your super-important work party where I'm going to finally
meet all of your coworkers because I need to stay home to spend
three hours writing an 11 Points list about the spelling mistakes on
street signs.

Of course, there's a reason behind this. Whether I'm thoughtful
or not, she really *wants* me to be thoughtful. *If I'm her ideal guy,
it means I'm thoughtful.* So maybe if she says it out loud, it'll
come true.[85]

**(4) She shows absolutely no sign of craziness or
baggage.** A woman knows you're on high alert for any signs of
craziness. It's *the* biggest gender stereotype ("All girls are crazy,
all men are assholes."). So *she's going to make sure that you
don't see even the slightest hint of madness*—at least not
until you're locked down and then she can be free to guzzle a bottle
of aspirin because she can't find her *Legally Blonde 2: Red, White
and Blonde* DVD.

(5) She references one of your jokes. Don't take it as a sign
if a woman seems to be laughing at all of your shitty jokes. That's a
skill that's ingrained into the female brain from thousands of years

---

[85]   This is doubly true if she cuts out your picture for her "secret" vision board and writes
"Thoughtful!" underneath it.

of evolution. The real sign she's madly in love with you is when *she integrates your shitty jokes into her vernacular.*

(6) She connects herself to delicious food. One of the wisest proverbs ever is, "The best way to a man's heart is through his stomach."[86] It's true, and not just for less-invasive angioplasties.

She knows that as much as you like her, *you'll like her even more if, every time you see her, you get to gorge on deliciousness.*

It's why any woman will happily make the trade of you getting a little bit chubbier for a commitment. She'll give you those last few bites of the dessert you're splitting. She'll just so happen to have baked a delicious batch of brownies when you come over. She'll fatten you up like you're Hansel and Gretel and, like that witch, will still let you spend time inside her sugar walls. (Too far?)

(7) She drinks heavily on a weekday. There aren't any numbers to back this up, but from countless observations, I believe men are more likely than women to see the joys of getting drunk on a Tuesday.

So if she's willing to throw caution to the wind and put down a full bottle of wine, work tomorrow be damned, it's a calculated move (calculated not being used pejoratively there). *She's calculated that getting all messed up on wine will lead to a crazier night,* lowered inhibitions, and more excuses for unexpected heavy petting.

Or she's an alcoholic.

(8) Her friends meet you, pretend they haven't heard a lot about you, and ask the questions she can't. Here's an exchange I had (paraphrased) when I met a friend of a girl I'd been dating for one month when said girl went to the bathroom:

---

[86] The worst proverb ever? "An apple a day keeps the doctor away." I have a friend with diabetes. If he eats an apple it destroys his blood sugar. Whoever wrote that proverb had no idea about carbs.

Friend: "So you like Beth,[87] huh?"

Me: "Yes, she's great."

Friend: "You're Jewish, right?"

Me: "Yes. Are you?"

Friend: "No, I'm black."

Me: "There are black Jews. And not just Sammy Davis, Jr., Whoopi Goldberg, and hall-of-famer Rod Carew (he converted). Ethiopian Jews. I met some of them when I was in Isr—"

Friend: "So would you be allowed to marry Beth even though she's not Jewish? What would your family think?"

Me: "*That's a pretty aggressive question* to be asking five minutes after I met you. And with the waitress standing at the table the whole time."

(9) She totally looks the other way on your crappy car, shitty friends, mismatched furniture, and other blatant red flags. Eventually the honeymoon period will wear off: she'll realize you've been picking her up in a 1994 LeBaron,[88] your friends are the kind of guys who go to strip clubs and think the strippers are actually into them, and your furniture could best be described as "a patchwork of soiling." And then, a lifetime of henpecking will begin.[89]

But until that happens, *she's willfully ignoring all of those very, very blatant red flags,* because there's something great that she sees in you that makes them look minor in comparison.

(10) She wears shoes that make sure you're taller. This isn't at play for everyone but, based on population-wide height statistics, this should apply to most. For me, standing at 5-foot-8 soaking wet, it was an incredibly accurate test.

---

87   Not actually her name.

88   And not even one that Jon Voight the actor *or* the dentist once drove.

89   I always knew this moment was coming when, about a month in, the girl I was dating would say, "So living with your three buddies, it's kinda like a frat house, huh?"

If I went on a date with a girl and she was wearing flats, I knew she was into me. If she was wearing heels, I knew it was a lost cause. It's simple. *Both women and men are more comfortable when the man is taller.* Subconsciously, a woman knows this. So when she's getting dressed, is she thinking about you? If she puts on heels that will make her taller than you—no matter how good they make her legs and buttocks look, no matter how well they match what she's wearing, no matter how out-of-style flats are—you weren't on her mind when she was getting dressed. If she sucks it up and puts on flats, she's sending the message that she wants you to be the man—standing tall, not being subtly emasculated for the entire night.

(11) She is available 100 percent of the time. In the "11 Signs a Guy's Into You" there was a grand, overall point: how he acts when he's not with you. This list has a grand, overall point, too: how she acts when you want her to be with you.

I'm about to share a truth that's sad and unfair and maddening—but still the truth. *When a woman's into you, she will ALWAYS have time for you.* You vault up to the number one priority on her list—ahead of work, ahead of hobbies, ahead of social plans, ahead of friends, ahead of family gatherings, ahead of everything.

You can use this to figure out, with irrefutable certainty, whether she's into you. If you ask her out and she's available the day you want—or has something unbreakable and frantically finds a replacement date—she likes you. If she isn't sure if she can do it that day, has a lot going on, might have a work thing, or, worst of all, cancels the date after it's made, she's not into you. She might not even realize it—it could be her subconscious doing the weeding out—but she's not. And if you keep pushing, you're in for frustration, irritation, disappointment, and sooner rather than later, her breaking it off.

11 Ways Modern Technology Can
Enhance Your Dating Life

This book was written during the summer of 2010. And while I hope a lot of the principles I'm presenting are timeless . . . the ones in this list are certainly a time capsule to this moment.

So if you're reading this way in the future—or not even reading it, just having it implanted in your brain by your robot butler to give you something to think about on your vacation to the moon—try not to judge me the way I'd judge a dating book from the 1980s talking about the seductive power of having a VCR at home, how to place the perfect personal ad in the newspaper, and how long-distance relationships will never work because the phone calls are too expensive.

(1) Facebook is the best noncommittal way to make contact in the history of mankind.[90] I hate asking women for their numbers. I've always felt the transition from talking to asking for a number is stilted . . . plus, I like leaving things a little ambiguous for the girl, not letting her know whether I'm interested or just a friendly guy.

Instead, I always make sure to casually drop Facebook into the conversation. Because it can lead to this exchange:

Me: *"Blah blah on Facebook blah blah joke blah."*

Her: *"Haha blah blah indulging my bad joke blah blah Facebook blah blah."*

Me: *"Are you on Facebook?"*

Her: *"Yep."*

---

[90] At least I assume. I have no idea if a strategic smoke signal or cave painting was better.

Me: *"Why aren't we Facebook friends then?"*

Her: *"Because we just met!"*

Me: *"Blah blah."*

Man, typing that out I can't believe it worked so well. We really do make women meet us more than halfway.

Anyway, that conversation, coupled with me getting her name, makes it so the next day I can add her as a friend on Facebook. With the friend request, I'll send a message like, "Since we weren't friends already for some reason, I'm requesting you now. Now don't screw me here." She accepts, and, if she's interested, she'll send a little message back to me. From there, we exchange Facebook messages for a while and eventually transition that into a date. It seems ridiculous, but it's proven to work. Repeatedly.

And sometimes it didn't, which was fine, too. Rather than ask someone for a number and have her say, "Oooh, I'm sorry, I don't give it out," the Facebook method diffuses and soothes the rejection process. *The friend-request-with-a-message is a perfect weed out.* If she's not interested, she'll sit on the request for a few days, and probably not write a message back. If that happens, it's fine—you just friend requested a person you met out (which people do all the time) and did not put yourself out there *at all.* She (or he, this works both ways) never has to know you were interested. And now you move on.

(2) Late-night texting. Late-night texting won't help your "dating life" as much as your "sex life," but it has redefined the concept of the booty call. Thanks to the texting explosion, the term "booty call" hasn't been accurate since it was the title of an underrated black comedy.[91]

---

[91] By black comedy I mean comedy featuring black people, not, like *Very Bad Things,* which was so bad that it couldn't have been saved even by replacing all the actors with much funnier black guys. Also, the movie *Booty Call* doesn't actually feature a booty call; it features a double date. But whatever.

It's all booty texting now.[92] I can't even imagine having to pick up the phone and call a woman to ask her to come over at 2 AM That sounds more uncomfortable than the scene in *Booty Call* where they tried to capitalize on Jamie Foxx's talents by having Vivica A. Fox tell him that impressions turn her on. (Seriously. That would've been like casting Michael Winslow in the role and having her say, "You know what turns me on? A guy who can make all kinds of sound effects.")

(3) Quick IM/e-mail/Twitter cameos can keep you on the person's mind. Calling someone to talk is committal. Sending a quick message over gChat, forwarding an e-mail, or re-tweeting his/her pithy observations about the quality of artwork in hotel rooms— *those keep you on the person's radar while keeping the thrill of the chase alive.* Once you're having hour-long phone calls, the chase is over.

(4) You can research the hell out of someone before a date. Between Google, Facebook, LinkedIn, and the residual MySpace, LiveJournal, or Friendster profile he/she still hasn't bothered to take down, *you can get a very thorough picture before you even go out on your first date.*

You can also run a few tests, like Googling the person's name alongside deal-breaker keywords like "sex offender registry" or "Movementarian cult."

(5) When you actually use old-fashioned communication, it means more. No matter how much I Facebook message, text, IM, and e-mail with a girl, when I'm going to ask her out, I do it by picking up the phone and calling her. This is very much by design.

We've all become so accustomed to the impersonal (or quasi-personal) modern modes of communication that the *older ones make a big impact.* It's why you're so impressed when you get

---

[92] And check out the booty call list in Chapter 4 for way more of a handbook on all this.

a handwritten letter now. Or why I forced my publisher to send me the contract for this book via Pony Express.[93]

By using old-fashioned communication—and, yes, a phone call counts as "old-fashioned"—you're subconsciously sending the message that *This Is Important, and You Are Important to Me.*

(6) You can video chat. I'm not sure if this is all *that* great— the verdict is still out on whether we actually *want* to look at people while we talk with them—but I do know that *it was one of the most anticipated aspects of The Future.* And now it's here. So enjoy, *Jetsons* enthusiasts.[94]

(7) Caller ID and voice mail give you great control. Ah, the old power struggle of dating. *Who has the upper hand?* Who is waiting on whom?

Caller ID and voice mail are big advantages. People who were dating 25 years ago just had to pick up the phone and ask, "Hello?" Now your cell phone rings, you see who's calling, and you can screen the call—either because you're not ready to talk, or because you want to make the person sweat.

(8) GPS makes sure your dates don't end with disastrous misadventures. I'm sure that getting lost on a date can turn into a really memorable night of bonding over shared adversity. Unless, of course, you end up driving off a cliff or into some backwoods area where you run out of gas, ask a local for help, and end up chained to a basement wall.

Still . . . *a date that goes smoothly is better than a date that doesn't.* For every memorable moment of shared adversity with your future boy/girlfriend, you'll have 15 "oh my God, the date

---

[93] Which almost turned out to be a horrible idea when the horses took a detour toward Eastwood Ravine.

[94] Video chatting is very useful when you're dating long distance. Check out the list "11 Keys to Making a Long-Distance Relationship Work" for all the nuances.

was a disaster, we didn't get along that well and on top of that we got *lost* and had to spend even more excruciating time together."

(9) Online dating is an incredible opportunity. I mean, at this point *I should probably just contact the big dating sites and ask them to send me money* for how much I've pimped them in this book. And we're only on the second chapter.

(10) All the person's photos online can be *so* amazingly informative. Whenever I start dating someone, I go through every single one of her photos online. Pictures are worth a thousand words, right? *So the treasury of photos online extrapolates out to so many words it's like Tolstoy wrote her biography.*[95]

(11) Movies on demand. During a date, some movie is going to come up. One of you hasn't seen it. The other one is shocked— *shocked*, I tell ya—that anyone hasn't seen such a mind-blowing movie.

Now, *you have the perfect late-night plan* (and perfect "let's put on a show to hide our intentions" excuse to go home together)—we're going back to my house to watch it. And if you don't own it, there are now 25 different ways to stream it to your TV. We're getting closer and closer to a point where every movie will be available to you anytime you want.

So use that to your advantage. And make sure he really appreciates the subtleties of *The Cutting Edge* or that she's paying close attention during the lamp speech in *The Jerk*.

---

[95] Or J. K. Rowling, from *Goblet of Fire* on. And in either case, Leon Uris wrote the foreword.

11 Ways Modern Technology Can
Ruin Your Dating Life

This list is a complement to the "11 Ways Modern Technology Can Enhance Your Dating Life" list. Because nothing that good in life is free.[96]

(1) Getting exposed on your Facebook wall. To this day, *I don't know how I got away with dating multiple people simultaneously in the age of Facebook.* One wall post from one girl saying, "Had a great time on our date last night" could've started a chain reaction that would've led to me being blackballed from like six different friend groups. But none of them ever did. It's like I was a party to some kind of miracle.[97]

(2) Ill-advised (and often intoxicated) texting. Whether you were *drunk, emotional, impulsive, or under duress, your cell phone doesn't care.* If you send a regrettable message, it's now permanent.

I'm definitely a drunk texter. It's bad. My strategy: If I really liked a girl, I would give her number to a friend, then completely delete her from my phone before a night out. I figured I'd get the number back the next day and be guaranteed not to cause any damage. It was like buying insurance on my lack of impulse control.

(3) Overcommunicating early on. There's a theory—one I don't fully subscribe to but that I think has case-by-case merits—

---

[96] Regardless of what Janet Jackson and Luther Vandross told us in their gift-to-mankind-from-God 1992 duet "The Best Things in Life Are Free."

[97] Which puts one checkmark in the "pro" column of my application for sainthood. If only every single other thing I've written in this book didn't fall under the "con" column. Oh, and the Jewish thing.

that says you should talk to someone as little as possible between meeting him/her and going on your first date. It all comes back to the old idea to "leave 'em wanting more."

When you meet someone and briefly charm that person enough to lead to a date, you've left him/her wanting more.

The more you communicate between that moment and the next time you're face-to-face, the less mysterious you are. Lose the mystery, and the other person might lose interest. It's like how I stopped watching *Law & Order: SVU* when I realized that the famous guest star is always the bad guy. That ruined the show for me. Sometimes it's better not to know.

(4) You can learn too much too easily. I know people who absolutely refuse to Google a person or look him/her up on Facebook before a date. *Part of the fun of dating is learning about the person*—and if you know his/her likes and dislikes, career history, college activities, and recent vacations from online research, that will leave you with only two options: (1) Cut every story off at the base by saying, "Yeah, I saw that on your Facebook profile," or (2) play dumb and channel your acting skills to feign surprise and interest.

In scenario one, you're a stalker. In scenario two, you're an untrained actor in a high-stakes situation, like Ice-T. And I'm not sure which is worse.[98]

(5) Making a date over text is very unromantic. Asking someone out over text is as *impersonal and unprofessional* as firing someone via a fax machine. Unless you're the boss in *Back to the Future Part II* who fires Marty via fax. He was a pro. And he video chatted. See, all anyone ever wanted from the future was video chat.

---

[98] Although, as stated just seconds earlier, I haven't watched *SVU* in a while, so maybe Ice-T's gotten better.

(6) No one looks good on video chat. Here's my problem with webcams and front-facing cell phone cameras: *They make us look terrible.* In low-resolution video without any form of proper lighting, no one can look their best.

When you're first dating someone, you put every possible effort into looking good. I rarely busted out my glasses until after a month of dating. Before every date I would shave extra carefully as to not nick up my face or, even worse, leave one stray facial hair for her to fixate on all night. Video chatting invalidates all of that effort. It's singlehandedly keeping the word "splotchy" in the English language.

(7) Your calls get screened, leaving you in the post-voice-mail purgatory. I'm going to do this one entirely in a tennis metaphor, just for kicks. Leaving a voice mail for someone you just started dating is as excruciating as when Monica Seles got stabbed. (Whoa! That escalated *quickly*.) Because it puts the ball entirely in that person's court. And you just have to stand there on the baseline, as useless as Anna Kournikova (but just as attractive, don't worry), waiting for the return.

And waiting for that volley back is agonizing.[99] You can't call again without getting one back first—that gives the other person *way* too much of an advantage over you (ad out). You're in deuce—a seemingly endless purgatory while you wait. I blame caller ID, call screening, and voice mail for standing in your way and making it so difficult to serve up what you really want . . . love.

(8) GPS makes you way too "findable." Forget that all the phones we carry have GPS built in, tons of different social networking services let you give constant updates on your location, and your GPS device in your car keeps a log of where you go. Next time you're on an airplane, flip through the SkyMall catalog—it's packed with *tiny GPS trackers someone can attach to your car* or throw

[99] I debated turning that word into Agassinizing but felt that was too Navritilover the top.

in your bag. Anyone with a little motivation—and the willpower to call SkyMall and *not* order a giant giraffe sculpture—can track your every move on the cheap.

(9) The ease of online dating leads to pitfalls. Online dating can be a place to meet an endless supply of people, taking you on any number of Internet-fueled sexy misadventures until the website finally hooks you up with someone who's perfect. It can also be a place where you find nothing but married men, women using photos from the previous decade, and socially inept misfits who only want to talk about how many eight-year-olds they could take in a fight.

That's why it will never replace face-to-face meetings; *it's just a supplement* (a really strong supplement, like the one everyone in baseball was taking in the late nineties—but still a supplement).

(10) Bad photos of you get tagged all the time. I love when I'm in the car with people and suddenly all the phones buzz at once. It's quickly followed by everyone checking and the simultaneous, "Oh goddammit, [some girl] just tagged me in a bunch of Facebook photos." Then there's *that period of horror between receiving that notification and actually seeing the photos* of you that have now been shared with the world.

(11) The death of mixtapes. There's a great scene in *High Fidelity* where John Cusack talks about giving girls mixtapes, and just what an important element they are in the art of seduction. *What can you do now?* Make a CD, like a caveman? Give a girl a list of 10 songs and an iTunes gift card? Tell her to type "Boyz II Men" into Pandora? Come on.

11 Translations of Key Phrases Women Say

This is the only time in this book I'm doing a list about one gender and not a counterpoint for the other gender. I think it's because guys are a little simpler to decode. Everything you need was summarized in the "11 Signs a Guy's Into You" list. For women, an entire extra list is needed. What can I say? Women are just the more complicated and coded gender. It's a part of what they teach in school on Venus.

(1) "We're definitely not having sex tonight."

Translation: *"We're probably going to have sex tonight."*

This one always cracked me up. By qualifying that sex is not an option, a woman not-so-subtly lets you know that you two are at the point where she *has* been considering sex as an option. In the shower before the date she shaved her legs, and not just up to the knee, telling herself "it's definitely not happening tonight, but, uh . . . we might end up swimming so they need to be clear. Yeah, swimming! That's why I'm doing this."

Of course, *now the burden falls to you not to screw it up.* And you might. You're the mountain climber on *The Price Is Right*, the yodeling music is playing, and everything you say and do pushes you closer and closer to falling off. But if you play smart and careful, it's right there waiting for you.[100]

(2) "I'm really low maintenance."

Translation: *"I'm really high maintenance."*

---

[100] Yes, in this metaphor being dangerous and exciting are the equivalent of making a good guess on what the price of a blender and a box of dishwashing soap cost. Just go with it.

It's been a lot of years since I took Intro to Shakespeare (and I wasn't paying particularly good attention at the time anyway— liberal arts requirements really got in the way of MarioKart) but I'll never forget that quote about a lady doth protesting too much.

Any time the woman you just met feels the need to explain how she is the über-appealing opposite of a negative female stereotype ("I'm low maintenance! I am just looking for something casual! I'm not crazy!") *she's dothing some serious overprotesting.*

(3) "You're so much less of an asshole than the guys I usually date."

Translation: *"Unless you show me some mind-blowing sexual chemistry later tonight I'm going to relegate you to 'just a friend.'"*

There's a reason that women since the dawn of time have dated a bunch of assholes.[101] Assholes provide everything they want during their "dating around" period: drama, mental torment, frustration, anger . . . and excitement, conquest, challenge, and passion.

After a particularly bad asshole relationship goes south, many women rebound to a nicer guy. He's not as handsome, not as dangerous, not as exciting, not as dashing (whatever that means). But he's so nice and chivalrous. He opens car doors. He calls to make sure she got home safely. He does little awkward things that are so charming.

She also has a 130-decibel alarm going off in her head at all times saying, "We are not going to have any sexual chemistry. This guy isn't going to rip my clothes off—he's going to take them off and fold them neatly on the bureau." So unless *you prove you can bring the fastball in bed as well as you bring the bouquet of flowers,* she's done with you.

---

[101] Even in the Bible. You think Noah didn't play mind games? And Joseph's coat was the original form of *Pickup Artist* peacocking.

(4) "I have to wake up early tomorrow for [anything work-related or any big event]."

Translation: *"I'm not optimistic about this date."*

See the "11 Signs a Woman's Really Into You" list—there's no way she would've let work or a social event interfere if she was optimistic about tonight spilling over into tomorrow. She would've worked overtime, rescheduled the call, or told the people planning the event she'd be late. *You're either first priority or you don't crack the priority list.* There's no silver or bronze medal—just the gold and the dreaded yellow participation ribbon.

(5) "I have to wake up early tomorrow for [a solo event, like running or baking stuff for a party]."

Translation: *"I'm 50–50 about this date."*

This is a different scenario. *She's hedging her bet here*—if she doesn't like the date, she can cut off any post-date shenanigans with an "I'm so sorry but I really have to run, I have this half-marathon in three weeks." If she does like the date, she can *really* impress you by blowing off her activity to . . . uh . . . I really wanted to do parallel sentence structure here, but my grandma's going to read this.

(6) "I never do this on a first date."

Translation: *"I've done this a couple of times before with guys like you—guys I'm more physically than mentally attracted to."*

Yes, that's right, her translation ends in a prepositional phrase. It happens. After all, *she's not mentally attracted to you, no reason to bring out the big grammar guns.*

(7) "I've heard good things about that place, sounds great."

Translation: *"I've actually never heard anything about that place, but I'm so happy that you actually took the time to plan something for our date that I'm going to validate the hell out of you."*

Little thoughtful gestures can be worth *way* more than you'd think. Other guys have set the bar so low that simply planning out a two- or three-activity date (instead of picking her up and saying, "So . . . uh . . . what do you wanna do?") turns her on. *Emotionally, not necessarily physically* (although maybe physically, if one of the activities you planned is mechanical bull riding or nude skydiving[102]).

(8) "I haven't been out partying like this in a *while*!"

Translation: *"I'm trying to show you I'm cool and I can hang, but I'm 100 percent over my partying phase and want no part of this if we get into a relationship."*

She's putting on her game face because she wants to impress you—and, to a certain degree, impress herself. But if she admits she hasn't been barhopping or out until three in the morning or to a nightclub in "a while" . . . it's because *she's done with that part of her life.*

You may be fine with that, by the way. You may be putting on a game face for her just as much. You may be reaching that point where going to dinner, then going home, watching half a movie, falling asleep by 11:30, and waking up with a clear head before the crack of 11:30 sounds pretty fantastic. Just know that if you're *not* there yet, it's going to cause some tension down the road once the relationship ages a little and some of the new romance shine wears off.

(9) "Oooh, you *don't* want to go down there right now."

---

[102] Though, if you're planning dates with activities like nude skydiving, you were probably a huge fan of the show *Blind Date*. Those dates couldn't have been more unrealistic: "I just met you, let's go make pottery, participate in a Civil War reenactment, and swim with military-trained dolphins." Meanwhile the postproduction crew has added a thought bubble over your head the whole time saying, "I'm a loser."

Translation: *"I never plan on seeing you again."*

This moment happens during a hookup that she wants to keep . . . well, not quite PG. Let's say PG as it's defined in Europe: topless-ness, some dry wit, and nothing more. So she plays the menstrual card. And that is the ultimate trump card, because *it's certain to stop everyone but a true pervert in his tracks.*

The reason I translate this to mean "I never plan on seeing you again" is because it puts an unsexy image in your head that's going to be very difficult to shake. She doesn't care, though, because she's done with you.

If she was going to see you again—and happened to be menstruating—she'd find any other way to slow you down. "Let's slow down, OK?"; "Next time"; "I like you, so let's hold off." Or, in lieu of talking, she'd perform the evasive body maneuver that all women somehow know. If she likes you, she doesn't want you associating thoughts about her cycle with one of your first moments of intimacy.

(10) "I've had sex with three people."

Translation: *"I've had sex with [zero to nine] people."*

"I've had sex with nine people."

Translation: *"I've had sex with [10 to 40,000] people."*

I have a theory that, if you ask a woman how many people she's had sex with (and she answers rather than asking you firmly to pull through to the next window to pick up your Frosty), there are only two responses you'll ever hear: three guys or nine guys.

She'll answer three if the real number is between one and nine. With three, she shows she's got a bit of experience, but she's other-wise very picky and chaste.

She'll answer nine if the real number is between 10 and 40,000. With nine, she can maintain *the mythical single-digit sex-partner number* (which seems to have been unofficially, but universally, established as the female promiscuity Mason-Dixon line), but still make it clear she'd had a few extra swings in the ol' batting cage.

(11) "So last night my friends were asking me, 'So what *are* you guys? Is he your boyfriend or what?' And I told them I hadn't really thought about it but it got me wondering, 'Yeah, what *are* we?'"

Translation: *"As much as I'm pretending to be laid back, not a moment goes by that I'm not stressing over the status of our relationship."*

She's *so* laid back, she hasn't been stressing about "Defining the Relationship." *It's those meddlesome, nosy friends of hers, of course.* But now that this topic was broached for the first time, it's going to keep coming up again and again and again. If only her friends weren't so damn persistent, right?

11 Answers for "How Long Should I Wait To Call?" Dilemmas

While I was writing this book, as a matter of policy, I banned myself from looking at other dating/relationships/sex books, magazines, and websites. I didn't want other ideas influencing me; my mission statement from day one was that nothing in this book would be recycled.[103]

But, just for sport, I Googled "how long should I wait to call?" I wouldn't read any of the results; I just wanted to pick up a range from the little Google summaries. And within five pages of results I found advice ranging from 24 hours to nine days. Clearly, it's a subject that everyone wants to talk about but no one agrees upon.

Well . . . since you bought this book (or took it out of the library like a freeloader), for now, you've implicitly decided to agree with me. And I take this responsibility very seriously. I stand with absolute gumption behind all 11 of the wait periods below. Gumption. Let's see dating-advice-help-guy-cool.com have *that*.

Two quick notes: (1) All of these scenarios apply when you're actually interested in the person you're communicating with. And (2) I always err on the side of communicating a little earlier than a little later—from my perspective, it's ultimately better to be perceived as a little too interested than flaky or unreliable.

---

[103] I even told the publisher to make sure not to print it on even 1 percent recycled paper. Sure, we'd have to kill a bunch of unnecessary trees, but the mission statement's the mission statement.

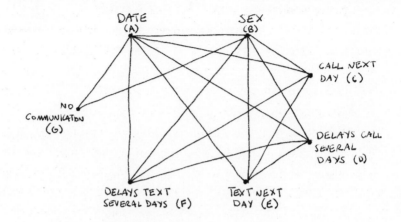

A̅B̅	SO THAT DATE WENT WELL, HUH?
A̅C̅	HE'S VERY INTERESTED IN YOU
A̅D̅	PLAYING IT COOL
A̅E̅	YOU'RE ON HIS MIND, BUT HE'S UNCONVINCED
A̅F̅	STRINGING YOU ALONG AS BACKUP
A̅G̅	IT'S OVER
B̅C̅	HE FEELS GUILTY ABOUT HOW IT WENT DOWN
B̅D̅	NOT INTERESTED, BUT AFRAID YOUR PATHS WILL CROSS
B̅E̅	WANTS A REPEAT, SOON
B̅F̅	BOOTY CALL
B̅G̅	ONE NIGHT STAND
C̅E̅	SO INTO YOU THAT HE'S FORGETTING FUNDAMENTALS
C̅F̅	WORRIED 'CAUSE YOU HAVEN'T CALLED BACK
D̅E̅	THE CALL IS TO ASK YOU OUT
D̅F̅	HAD MAJOR CRISIS AND WANTS TO EXPLAIN*
	* = VERY, VERY RARE CASE

(1) After you get someone's number. If you're going to call, wait two days. It's *enough time to build a bit of uncertainty but still keep both of you excited*—and to make sure you don't have to open the call feeling like you have to describe who you are.[104]

---

[104] Extend to three days if you'd end up calling on a Friday or Saturday. The whole point in putting off a call is to subconsciously send the message that you rock and roll all night and part of every day. Calling on a weekend belies that—I mean, how did you have time to call when you clearly

If you're going to text, there's no reason to wait any longer than the next night. Whether it's a "hey I met you last night and just saw [reference to some movie/ad/sport we talked about]" text or a "what are you up to tonight? We're going to [someplace]" text, might as well get things moving. Texting comes off as much less serious and much lower pressure, so there's no real benefit in waiting.

(2) After you get a text. After you get the first text from someone, wait about 15 minutes from when you see it to respond. You probably saw it instantly. Most people constantly check their phones—as if you're Jack Bauer waiting to get a life-or-death "the Russian ambassador has been kidnapped by generic Middle Eastern terrorists who are secretly working for your evil half-uncle" message from the president, and not just a message from Verizon telling you your bill is available online. Wait a little bit, let the person have a little time to sweat, but *text back quickly enough to make it clear that you're receptive to starting this dialogue.*

From that point on, let the other person's pace dictate your response time. You don't gain any edge if he/she is texting back instantly and you're waiting five minutes every time; all you're doing is screwing up the pace of the conversation.

(3) After you miss a call. The most agonizing time is the period between leaving a voice mail and waiting for a callback. So, naturally, this is the time when *you get to completely mind-intercourse the person* who called you.

Wait a minimum of two hours . . . but make sure that you call back the same day (and before 10:30 PM). Any shorter and you lose the opportunity to raise the person's interest by gently toying with his/her fragility. Any longer and you're just kind of annoying . . . and that window of agony will transition into resentment.

---

decided to hop on a last-minute flight to Rio for a 48-hour techno- and guarana-fueled bender?

(4) After you meet someone and want to do a Facebook friend request. Do it the next afternoon, or before the weekend is over at the latest. And when you're friend requesting him/her, make sure to request a few other people, too—you just so happen to be friending some of the lovely people you met this weekend. *If you wait any longer it seems less casual* and more calculated. And since you're going the ultra-cowardly Facebook route to seem casual and not put yourself out there at all, might as well fully commit to that façade.

(5) After you get an e-mail. Wait about an hour. That shows you're down for getting a dialogue going. And when you write your message, *make sure you ask at least two or three direct questions.* You want to open the door for the person to write back.[105]

(6) After a text later than 1:20 AM. At this hour, there *really isn't time for games.* If you want to find yourself heading to his/her place (or him/her coming over to yours), text back quickly. If you just want to get a good night's sleep—to spread out in bed, let the Taco Bell you just ate have its way with your system unabated, and not have to take a shower and do a five-minute grooming touch-up[106]—text back the next day.

(7) After a good first date. This one is a guy thing because, political correctness aside, the after-date call is pretty much always

---

[105] But be careful on this first one not to use words that might get you flagged as spam. He/she probably won't be regularly checking the spam folder just in case you write back. So watch out for words and phrases like Viagra, credit score, erectile, Xanax, or horny Russian girls. Honestly, if you *were* going to use any of those in your initial e-mail back, I'd be pretty impressed.

[106] This includes light deodorant, tooth brushing, and removal of any major unsightly body hair. For a woman it also includes shaving legs. Sorry.

squarely on the guy's shoulders. Apologizes to Susan B. Anthony; I'm just trying To B. Truthful.[107]

If the date was good—and you think there's some real potential there—you need to call the next day. It sends a powerful message about your interest . . . and even if she really *wishes* she could use any perceived overeagerness on your part to gain the power, her girl instincts will force her to swoon.

(8) After a second date. After the first date, you should get in touch quickly; after a second date, even a great one, it's worth it to give an extra day or two for a cooling-off period. Basically, you want him/her to have a couple days of thinking about you but not having access to you. It *makes you much, much more desirable* that way. Letting the other person's imagination run wild is doing you more favors than a phone call ever could, regardless of how much your wit sparkles.[108]

(9) After the first time you have sex. You have to call, on the phone, before dinner the next day. At least *if you want there to be a second time.*

(10) After a one-night stand. This is weird ground because you met someone, made some controversial choices that same night, and now you're faced with the dilemma of whether or not you should ever talk to him/her again.

If you decide not to call, this is, clearly, moot—it was a one-night stand that will not become a two-night sit(utation). But if you decide you want to text, *anytime in the next several days is fine.* Think about what you want to say, though; it's a bit gauche to follow up sex with "It was great meeting you."

---

[107] Somehow I couldn't get the phrasing on this joke right when I had Sojourner Truth in there. I'm just as surprised as you are.

[108] Even if your wit sparkles more than Edward Cullen taking his shirt off in direct sunlight.

(11) After it's been a week of radio silence and you want to give it one more shot. So you've gone out a few times, and you've been texting, talking on the phone occasionally, the usual. Then, one day, the communication stops. A week later, you still haven't heard from him/her and you start running through the scenarios. Maybe he texted and it didn't go through and he thinks *you're* the one who's gone silent. Maybe she had a death in the family. Maybe his phone got stolen, and he has no way to contact you. Maybe she was on a plane that crashed onto a mysterious island inhabited by evil spirits, polar bears, and tons of red herring.

Of course, none of those is the case. Maybe one out of 5,000 times one is. But the other 4,999 times, he/she just lost interest and figured you guys had been dating for a short enough time that no "I'm ending things" talk was necessary.

But you *have* to give it that shot. You won't be able to stop thinking about it until you do. In this case, *call on the ninth day.* When there's no answer, hang up without leaving a voice mail and send a text. Your voice mail will never be returned, but there's an outside chance your text will—you know, once she gets out of that coma.

11 Ways to Date a Coworker (Even Your Boss) without Things Getting Weird

Back when I first moved to Los Angeles, to make ends meet I got a job doing Web design for a travel website. A few weeks in, this absolutely gorgeous temp started working there—but gorgeous in a somehow approachable way (Mila Kunis gorgeous, not George Clooney gorgeous). I would frequently stop by her desk and talk with her . . . as would pretty much all of the other dudes in the office.

My coworker and new friend Matt (who was married, so not part of the Intern Derby) pulled me aside one day after he heard me ask her what she was up to that weekend. "Are you trying to dip your pen in the company ink?" he asked me. I stared blankly at him. I'd never heard that expression before. He reiterated, "You could be risking your job if you dip your *pen* in the company *ink*." More blank stares. "Your pen is your penis."

I didn't end up dating her. But at least I learned a new rule of life. Now here are 1,400 or so words on how to completely ignore that rule.

(1) Ask yourself: Would I be willing to lose my job for this person? You probably won't get fired because of an office romance, even a failed one. The probable worst-case scenario is that you'll have a bad breakup and wind up interacting only on a cold, terse, professional level. But in case something goes really, *really* wrong—like, say, you've grossly misinterpreted his/her interest level and you end up getting popped for sexual harassment—would you be willing to lose your job for this person? Possibly even getting blackballed in your field?

If your answer's yes, then go for it. If your answer's no, then you're just being too lazy to go find a quality boy/girlfriend elsewhere. And there's no place for that laziness in the American workplace.

(2) Test the waters with a work lunch. It could be fairly disastrous if you're looking at your coworker and thinking, "I think we want to date each other" and he's looking back at you thinking, "My, Tonya from customer service sure seems friendly." So *before you try to take things to another level, start out with lunch.*[109] Go someplace where you can talk, one-on-one, outside the office. That way, you can see if it feels like you're flirting with each other, or if you're just coworkers who have a good innocuous rapport when you bump into each other in the 12:30 microwave line.

(3) Don't tell one coworker until you're ready to tell 'em all. *Every office I've ever worked in feeds off gossip.* It's like every day you're a part of the most boring episode of *TMZ* ever.

Usually it's gossip about when the next fire drill is going to be or that someone overheard the vending machine guy saying he's going to start stocking a different brand of granola bars. Riveting stuff.

So if it's gossip about two coworkers shacking up, that's going to be the most exciting thing that happens in the office all year. Even your closest office friend isn't going to be able to keep that one a secret.

(4) Go ahead and hook up at the office. Why not? Assuming there aren't any security cameras, it's before or after hours, and there's no chance of you getting caught by a higher-up, *might as well cash in on one of the best perks of dating someone you work with.* But do it on a desk, not on the plush chairs in

---

[109] You could also organize an after-work happy hour. If the interest is reciprocated, he/she will be at that happy hour.

the reception area. For some reason, love stains show up extra well under harsh fluorescent office lights.

(5) Make sure you've got good (or, at least not really bad) long-term intentions. Coworkers are not a good pool for random one-night stands. You shouldn't date multiple coworkers simultaneously. (And no, you can't justify that to yourself as creating corporate synergy.)

Coworkers are a good pool for long-term relationships with an outside shot at marriage potential. It completely ruins a one-night stand if you see each other the next day stealing pens from the same office supply cabinet.[110]

(6) The Christmas Party Exemption. I first learned about the Christmas Party Exemption when I watched the movie *Scrooged*. There's a scene in there where Bill Murray goes to his office's Christmas party and one of the women there is sitting on the copy machine, Xeroxing her stuff. And even though the movie was made in the eighties and sexual harassment hadn't really been invented yet, I knew something seemed inappropriate there.

But it wasn't. Because it happened at the Christmas party. For whatever reason, *people seem really, really forgiving about behavior at the Christmas party.* So if there is a coworker who you have some good sexual tension with—but both of you know it would never go anywhere—it's probably Christmas party or never. Something about drinking company-sponsored liquor and getting a gift card to Target in a Secret Santa drawing just gives everyone an open mind.

(7) Don't feel bad talking about work on your dates. On your first date, there's going to be a point in the conversation

---

[110] Also, while you shouldn't home-wreck in day-to-day life, you especially shouldn't home-wreck in an office. There's no way that getting with a married coworker is going to work out cleanly. Not even if you both think Ziggy's gotten too preachy.

where you start talking about work. And after a few minutes one of you is going to say, "Ahh! Let's not talk about work." And then you'll both uncomfortably, frantically scan your brains, desperate for a new conversation topic . . . but one won't come fast enough and this deathly pause will set in, during which you'll both wonder if you have any connection *except* work.

You do. And you can relax. It's a first date. You both so badly want a subject where you can talk and laugh and feel comfortable. *Work is common ground.* Let the conversation take its natural course and, as you get to know each other better, you'll have an infinite amount of other subjects you want to talk about.[111]

(8) Make sure you have a backup set of work clothes on hand. If a date goes *extra* well and you end up spending the night together, you can't show up to the office the next day in the same outfit as you did the day before (or in your date outfit, which probably isn't workplace appropriate).

So make sure you have access to work clothes—*you "just so happen" to have some in your trunk.* And if you just so happen to have deodorant, contact solution, and a toothbrush, that's even better. How lucky that you randomly happened to throw all those things in your car the other night, right?

(9) If you're dating someone you manage, keep very, very careful statistics on work performance. That's right: You didn't just get yourself a boy/girlfriend . . . you just got yourself a brand-new bookkeeping project! When it comes time to discuss raises or promotions, *you better have damn good, quantifiable statistics that show exactly why this person deserves*

---

[111] If you meet someone on a World of Warcraft message board, then go out on a date and talk about World of Warcraft, that's totally logical. That's your common ground. For you, work is your World of Warcraft. Just way less cool, believe it or not.

extra money, or, more important, has earned the job over other candidates.[112]

If you do give him the promotion, you can guarantee everyone in the office is going to jump to the conclusion of "Well, shit, maybe I could've gotten the promotion if I'd just tossed it in her a few times." If there are numbers out there backing up your decision, at least the other people will only think that's 99.9 percent of the reason instead of the full 100.

(10) Be transparent with the HR department. Make sure to fill out any and all required paperwork and forms, especially if your relationship is a boss-employee situation. By keeping things on the up-and-up early, you avoid any possible issues later on. Plus, if marriage has taught us anything, it's that *nothing says romance like filling out a bunch of legal documents.*

(11) Whatever you do, break up amicably. No matter how much you're ready to go off, you should do your best to keep things peaceful. *You won't get the separation that normally comes with a breakup.* The next day you have to wake up, walk into a room, see him/her, and interact on a responsible, mature level.

But if that sounds completely unpalatable to you, get your résumé together, secure another job, and completely flip your shit during the breakup.

Here's a quote for you: "Sometimes you can't get over being hurt until you know you've been heard. Give yourself permission to express your anger and sadness." And you know who said that? Dr. Phil.[113]

---

[112] And if you're going to deny your boy/girlfriend a raise or promotion, you'd better have *twice* as thorough stats, because your statistic for "amount of tension in your relationship" is about to hit its new all-time high.

[113] That small-penised goon.

3

Dating

My car was stolen on a first date.

It was also the worst date of my life, as, somehow, it managed to bring about *11* separate misfortunes. Eleven! Sure, three misfortunes, that could happen to anyone. Seven, there's an outside chance. But 11 misfortunes? I never thought I'd see that . . .

Misfortune #1. I met the girl a few weeks earlier at speed dating. Yes, my friends and I went speed dating. Yes, I tried to go on a real date with someone I'd met there. And no, that doesn't technically make it our second date. Anyone who counts each of their three-minute speed dating conversations as "dates" is the kind of person who quantifies everyone on Facebook as "friends."

Misfortune #2. I made the ill-advised suggestion that we go to dinner, contradicting the time-tested rule that you shouldn't do a meal on a first date.

Misfortune #3. Her name was Natalie. I remember her name only because, in a move that I thought was charming at the time but, in retrospect, was *definitively* not, I suggested we get dinner at a restaurant called Natalee Thai. The restaurant was in Beverly Hills, but the less chic part of Beverly Hills—probably where Andrea Zuckerman lived. Paparazzi are not camping out near Natalee Thai.

Misfortune #4. When I scheduled the date for "next Monday," I failed to realize that was March 17th . . . subsequently ruining both of our St. Patrick's Day plans.

Misfortune #5. She was a half hour late to the date.

Misfortune #6. When she finally got there, I realized that the lighting at the speed dating bar was fuzzily dim . . . she now appeared about 10 years older than I expected or remembered.[114] Not a real problem—I've dated women born anywhere from 1969 to 1989, and been able to talk eighties music with all of them—but it caught me off guard.

Misfortune #7. Most of our terrible dinner was spent with her trying to get me to use the ultra-spicy Thai sauce and me refusing. Eventually I acquiesced—all those regrettable improv classes I took taught me that the only way to keep a scene moving is to say "Yes, and . . ." to any request. It was disgusting. The Thai sauce, not improv. Although I don't really like improv very much, either.

Misfortune #8. Of all nights to have bad service, it had to happen on this one. An absentee waitress made the date stretch to two painful hours.

Misfortune #9. Our conversation was brutal, as it quickly became clear we were in diametrically opposed places in life. She was clearly in a state that my friends and I would later call HusbandWatch '08; I was just out of a relationship and trying to have my way with every woman who came within an 11-foot radius.

Misfortune #10. After I paid the bill, we exchanged a quick *handshake* and walked in opposite directions to our cars. It was clear that

---

[114] An especially impressive feat considering she was Asian. You know that phrase "black don't crack"? I've been trying to popularize its Far East cousin, "Asians ain't agin'"—with limited results.

a love connection had not been established. A *hug* connection hadn't even been established. And I'll hug anything.

Misfortune #11. This is the biggest misfortune of all. I wandered the streets for 30 minutes looking for my car. I couldn't find it. Eventually I called the police and reported it missing. Two days later I was woken up by a call from the LAPD. They'd found my car in South Central L.A., stripped.

Yep. While I was sitting there, fighting off spicy Thai sauce and wondering if I should make a push to at least try to get a make-out session from this horrid date, some guys stole my 2004 Jeep Wrangler off the streets of Beverly Hills.[115]

It took no less than 200 hours of phone calls over the next few weeks to try to get the car towed back up to me and to get the insurance squared away. The car was covered but, unfortunately, my laptop inside was not.[116]

Anyway, during the process, I was so preoccupied that I never contacted Natalie again. I didn't want to go on another date with her, but I didn't even send a text to be polite. I assume she has no idea why I never contacted her (unless, of course, it was an inside job—even though the police never bothered to investigate, I still haven't entirely ruled that out).

There *is* a silver lining in all of this, though. For me, that date was rock bottom. They all went up from there. And the same thing

---

[115] I guess that these thieves just wanted to know what it was like to bump in a Jeep, which is why they completely ignored all of the Audis, BMWs, and Infinitis lining the street.

[116] I did two lists on my website about the things the car thieves chose to take from my car and the things they chose to leave behind. They took: my laptop, 20 cents worth of pennies, my $15 sunglasses, my writing notebook, and my incredibly crappy Bluetooth earpiece. They left: my real glasses, the awful radio, my Michael Vick–branded football, my license plates, and some of my mix CDs.

will happen to you. When you're sitting there on your worst date ever, just remind yourself that they all go up from here.

This chapter is all about dates: where to go, what to say, what to wear, how to prepare, how not to get your car stolen. Well, maybe not the last one; but, in theory, assume it's sort of an implicit side effect of following all the other advice.

11 Ideas for Fun, Memorable Dates

I'm not going to tell you to go to a cocktail lounge, or bowling alley, or private jet trip to the French Riviera. Those are obviously your go-to dates. I put this list together for those times when you're trying to think of something different to do for a date and you're drawing a gigantic blank.

(1) Wine tasting. In this book's continuing tradition of promoting *a connection between moderate amounts of alcohol consumption and dating success,* I present wine tasting. Even if there aren't wineries in your area, stores and restaurants have started figuring out that people like wine tasting, so you should be able to find one somewhere.

Not only is it a fun date, but it's the classiest possible way to get kinda wobbly on a Saturday afternoon.[117]

(2) A hike/picnic combo. I'm surprised more people don't go on hikes for dates. *I think it's because the word "hike" can be prohibitive.* Unless you're a hard-core outdoor adventurer or a Cambodian laborer, "hike" means "walk up a tree-lined gradual incline."

So pack some sandwiches, maybe some hummus, throw 'em in a picnic basket, keep said picnic basket away from the bear intelligentsia, and walk up a tree-lined gradual incline until you find a spot to stop and eat.

---

[117] Even more wobbly than taking a day trip to Space Camp. Remember when that was the grand prize on every episode of *Double Dare*? I never understood how having the ability to dig a flag out of a vat of refried beans qualified a kid to become a future astronaut.

(3) Train. Get on a train and travel somewhere an hour or two away. It doesn't matter where—the train is really the focus. Most trains today have dining cars, club rooms, bars, and an almost negligible amount of hobos with bindles. It's a unique experience and one that always ends with you saying, *"Man, I should take trains more often."*

As an alternative, you can try the bus date, as featured in the movie *40 Days and 40 Nights*.[118] This is a date where you get on a bus (or subway, or streetcar, or light rail, or, if you live in North Haverbrook, monorail) and just hang out there. You see the city, you people watch, and, if the movie is to be believed, it's just nonstop laughs. I've never had the balls to try this date and you've got to be as cocksure as Josh Hartnett to go for it—it's definitely high risk, high reward.

(4) An outdoor concert. Much better than an indoor concert. Even if you don't know or like the music being played, *just being outdoors surrounded by people and trees and the potential to roam free makes everything OK.* Indoor concerts somehow lack that element. If you don't like the music, you feel trapped.

You can pick an outdoor concert venue where you bring a blanket, listen to some Sousa, and see fireworks; where it's lesser-known local bands playing at an event in the park; or where it's Survivor, Mr. Big, or five-ninths of Def Leppard performing at the county fair.

---

[118] A movie that I enjoy despite its completely absurd premise. Josh Hartnett decides not to have sex or masturbate for 40 days (for Lent) and, in the process, goes absolutely crazy because he can't handle it. First of all, he exists in a world where wet dreams don't exist. Second of all, come on. Third of all, SPOILER ALERT, he ends up losing his vow at the last minute when his ex-girlfriend rapes him—honest to God, rapes him. And his new girlfriend's reaction to her boyfriend being raped isn't to call the police or SVU or ask him if he's OK; it's to become furious with him. And yet, in spite of the fact that I just boiled this movie down to "guy ridiculously goes insane just by not ejaculating for five-and-a-half weeks and gets raped but no one cares," I kinda like it. Damn you, Hollywood's second golden age.

(5) A tourist trap. I live in L.A. but spend almost no time on Hollywood Boulevard. I can bike to the Santa Monica Pier but I've only been there two or three times (and never ridden its Ferris wheel). I've never purchased a map of the stars' homes, been to a sitcom taping, OD'd on cocaine at Chateau Marmont, or stood in line for *The Price Is Right.*[119]

While you'd never go to those really tourist-y things on the average day, they're perfect for dates. You'll have a surprisingly good time (*places don't become tourist traps by being boring*), plus you'll find yourselves brought together by appreciating it in an ironic, cheesy, I-can't-believe-we're-here-but-now-that-we-are-can-we-get-funnel-cakes? way.

(6) A friend's play or band gig. Everyone's got a friend who plays music or does local theater (definitely spelled "theater" not "theatre" in this case). It's actually kind of slick to take your dates to these shows for four reasons:

(1) You're taking him/her around your friends, which sends positive signals. (2) You show that you're a supportive friend—your date doesn't need to know that you'd never, ever, ever sit through the community theater's performance of *Stop the Planet of the Apes (I Wanna Get Off)* if you weren't trying to get in his/her pants. (3) *If the show's good, your date will be impressed; if it's brutal, you can whale on it together.* And (4) your performing friend will always have some place to go afterward (a bar, a restaurant, whatever), so your date can organically move to a second location.

(7) Street festival. This is another one of those dates that combats the nearly universal mantra: *"We live in this city with so many things to do but we never do any of them."* If you search around, almost every weekend you can find street festivals,

---

[119] I have eaten at the same little chicken-and-salad restaurant two blocks from my house at least 400 times though, so, ya know.

tastes of Little Italy, traveling carnivals, block parties, parades, and snake hunts in Irelandland going on.

A lot of the dates on this list involve a lot of walking and talking, and that's by design—I find that having conversations on the move always feel less pressured and looser than sitting at a restaurant, staring at each other across a table, self-consciously worrying about where you're putting your elbows.[120]

Plus, at a street festival there'll probably be an opportunity to play carnival games to win your date a giant stuffed bear. And even though your parents were frugal and didn't let you play those games growing up, remember, you make your own money now . . . and they're nowhere in sight. It's totally worthwhile spending $20 to try to use a hollowed-out softball to knock down three lead-filled milk bottles.[121]

(8) Bingo. You'll probably need another activity afterward but, trust me, if there's one rule of life I know for a fact, it's this *Everybody. Loves. Bingo.* It's more universally loved than Raymond and not Chris. I don't know why. Bingo just hits something in our brains. It's like the fifth taste bud that only responds to MSG in Chinese food. No one knows why the body singles out things the way it does.

Even if you're sitting there reading this saying, "Bingo? I don't play bingo. This guy's an idiot," just go find a bingo hall (or nursing home) and play. You'll love it. And even though the old people there

---

[120] Having walk-and-talk conversations could also make you feel like you guys are starring in an Aaron Sorkin show, which is not without its charms.

[121] I can't even tell you how much it changed my life when I came to this realization. It was Christmas 2005. I was in Reno (of all places—long story) with my friend Adam and his now-wife Alicia and we wandered into Circus Circus. We wanted to play games and win toys. We both simultaneously realized our practical, a-penny-saved-is-a-penny-earned parents weren't around, and we both had jobs and disposable income. We dropped at least $50 on carnival games that night, walked out of Reno with two dozen stuffed animals, and have been talking about it ever since.

will be pros who can manage 15 cards at once while you sit there struggling going, "Wait . . . shit . . . did he already call N-41?" that just makes it sweeter when you win and take home money they would've used to buy bananas or perms. (Or medicine.)

(9) Mall pub crawl. Go to the biggest mall around and make it an all-day pub crawl. Go from restaurant to restaurant and have a drink at each one. *Chain restaurants are the best*—it will be the only time in your life you do a bar crawl from Chili's to Hooters to Flingers to TGI Friday's. (At least it *should* be the only time in your life you to that. That's a whole lot of flair to encounter more than once.)

(10) A dive bar strip club. There are plenty of strip clubs out there that are actually dive bars that just so happen to have semi-nude women—or men—wandering around inside.[122] So if you're going out with a woman who has a great sense of humor and no pretentiousness—or you're a woman who wants to *impress a guy with the most badass date any woman's ever planned* for him—go to a dive bar/strip club. At a minimum, you will *not* run out of things to talk about.

(11) Crash a wedding. *Wedding Crashers* is certainly a movie with some funny bits, but I had one major fundamental issue with it. The movie starts with a 10-minute montage of wedding crashing then spends the next 90 minutes at a stately manor off the coast of Maryland.

It would've been like calling *Scream* something like *Drew Barrymore's Popcorn Cook-off and Phone Call Extravaganza.*

---

[122] The greatest one of these is the Claremont Lounge in Atlanta. In my opinion, it's the single-most important thing to visit in that entire city. You can see Coca-Cola being bottled anywhere. But where else can you see obese middle-aged strippers who have to feed dollars in the jukebox just to have songs to dance to? Here in L.A., Jumbo's Clown Room is a close second.

So if you are going to crash a wedding, only watch the first 12th of that movie for guidance—and *actually crash a wedding*. You know the spots in town (banquet halls, fancy hotels, botanical gardens, and in some really special towns, Walmarts) where people throw the most massive weddings and parties. Get dressed up, buy a gift,[123] show up, and look like you know what you're doing. Then *eat some food, have some drinks, enjoy some dancing, and duck out before the crowd dwindles too much.*

It's a great time; plus it's exhilarating having that ever-so-slight risk that someone's going to expose you and throw you out of the building like Uncle Phil throwing Jazz.

---

[123] Buying a gift is a crucial element in this process. By bringing a gift, even if it's a $15 clock radio you picked up at CVS on the way, you're no longer expecting something for nothing—which absolves you morally (to a degree). Also, if you walk in with a huge wrapped box in your arms, no one's going to give you even half of a suspicious glance. It's win-win.

11 Date Ideas That Will Backfire Brutally

You know the sign that a date's backfiring. Your date has his/her arms folded, keeps checking the time, keeps yawning, and keeps telling you nothing's wrong. If you have to *ask* if something's wrong, everything's wrong. And in these 11 situations, all the ingredients are there to make things go very, very wrong.

(1) Comedy club. For the few years that I was a stand-up comedian, I performed in and/or attended at least 1,000 shows. And there's one irrefutable law I found: If you're at a comedy club on a date, the comedian on stage is somehow going to track you down—and fixate on you. Comics have incredible radar for nervous couples.[124]

And while his banter with you may or may not be funny—"Why are you on a date with this guy? He must have a huge penis. Does he? Does he have a huge penis? I bet it looks like a big pink can of Pringles. What's the deal with Pringles coming in the same kind of can as tennis balls? I don't know whether to eat them or *serve* them"—no matter what, it's going to make at least one of you just want the date to be over *now*.

Going beyond that, a date is a time to show off *your* charming personality and hilarious observations. *It doesn't do any good to go to a place where you can't talk to each other* and just have to sit there listening to someone else being funny.

(2) A date without a plan. There's nothing worse than having your date get in the car, looking over and saying, "So . . . where do

---

[124] And free food.

you wanna go?" *A bad date where you put a lot of effort into a plan is much better than any date without one.*

I always approached dates like I'd approach a trip to the barber. Before I go to the barber, I have a pretty good idea of what I want. Because if the barber says, "What kind of haircut do you want?" and I say, "I don't know, what do you think?" I could walk out of that place with some kind of bowl cut/shaved sides combo that makes me look like an extra in a community theater production of *Of Mice and Men*. When you don't plan out a date in advance, it's the equivalent of giving your date a Depression-era Dust Bowl haircut.

(3) Your friend's party. Your date doesn't know anyone. You know everyone. Ideally, she would walk into the party, hear a Jay-Z song is on (yes, a Jay-Z song is on), put her hands up, and have the butterflies fly away. (And probably start nodding her head/moving her hips like yeah, too.)

In reality, though, *she's going to end up clinging to your side the whole night*—especially if she sees everyone's in stilettos and she didn't get the memo—which is no fun for either of you. Going to a party anywhere in the USA can work after you've been on some dates, but on the first few dates, you need to be talking to each other.[125]

(4) A bar that's not your scene. When I take girls to bars, I look for three things: (1) A place I've been before; (2) a place where we can sit down and talk without "Rock You Like a Hurricane" blasting like we're at an air show; and (3) a place where we can get in without waiting in line. So I would never arrange a date at a hipster bar where you have to wait in a long line in an unmarked alley and give the doorman a secret password . . . then, when you finally get it, everyone's drinking oxygen-infused green tea brandy out of bowler hats.

---

[125] If, for no other reason, than to find out whether there are seven things he/she hates about you.

What makes me comfortable may differ from what makes you (and your date) comfortable, but use the transitive property on the principle. *Stick within your comfort zone so you're not self-conscious and uneasy the entire time.* Because, like dogs and bees, your date can smell fear.[126]

(5) An overnight trip. You need to *save overnight trips* until you really know him/her. If you try to bust out a romantic getaway to a quaint cabin upstate somewhere but, during the drive up, you make a joke about watching out for bears and she says, "My dad was mauled to death by a bear"—you've just ensured the longest weekend of both of your lives. It's definitely one of those occasions where you order your steak extra rare and pray for E. coli.[127]

(6) Massages or a day spa. If it's too early on to get a couples massage,[128] then a trip to a spa means *you're segregated to different areas for hours.* That's not a date.

Also, massages are surprisingly anti-sexual. Even though you're naked with someone rubbing you, massages (at least ones that aren't at parlors next to truck stops or pawnshops) generally don't lead to sexual arousal. A professional massage should feel so good that it provides the body with a euphoria that's totally different than an orgasm. And many people won't want that feeling tarnished by rolling around for some fifth-date we-still-don't-know-each-other's-bodies fornicating.

(7) Errands. I've been on two dates where the girls used them as an opportunity for some errands. And both times I stood there thinking, "You thought our date was going so bad that *errands*

---

[126] Yes, I know that fact because of the kid in *Jerry Maguire.* It's also how I know the human head (allegedly) weighs eight pounds.

[127] You could also try ordering your chicken breast "rare." I don't know if they'll do that, but remember: If it's shiny and pink on the inside, salmonella might set you free.

[128] And I assure you, if you're wondering if it's too early on to get a couples massage, it's too early on to get a couples massage.

would liven it up?" One time the girl asked if we could go to a drug-store, and she spent 45 minutes buying random crap. The other time—even stranger—the girl brought her taxes along in case we passed a post office where she could drop them off. It was January. She wasn't in that much of a rush.

Dates are not a time to grab a few things you need at Target, pick up some dry cleaning, prematurely mail in your taxes, or swing by your AA meeting. The person you're with *cleared his/her schedule to do something fun with you.* So it's inconsiderate to bring him/her along on errands . . . or, worse, turn him/her into your chauffeur. And don't try to sell it as "I planned an amazing scavenger hunt date for us! First we are going to go to Target and compete to see who can buy something whose name rhymes with either pleoderant or shmelve pack of Diet Coke."

(8) A long, sincere walk on the beach. There's a never-ending battle between good cheesy and bad cheesy.[129] Bad cheesy is going for a long walk on the beach, gazing into each other's eyes, comparing the beauty of a sunset to the beauty of the girl you're with, touring the bridges of Madison County, or ordering one milk-shake and two straws.[130]

Good cheesy is doing any of those things . . . but acknowledging that it's cheesy and making fun of your-self. So a long, sincere walk on the beach is bad cheesy. A long walk on the beach where you say, "If you're lactose intolerant, you'd better take your pills before this date" is good cheesy.

---

[129] It's real hard-core—as long-lasting as the battle between North Korea and South Korea, Bart Simpson and Sideshow Bob, Marvel and DC. Picture the intensity of those battles, but add in some John Mayer background music, and you get good cheesy versus bad cheesy.

[130] However, ordering an assortment of good cheeses isn't cheesy. Nor is ordering Cheetos, no matter what propaganda Chester Cheetah has been telling you.

(9) A sales pitch. I had a friend who got involved in a pyramid scheme to sell knives. She needed to sell knives and recruit other people to sell knives. She went on Match.com specifically to find guys to take to presentations about the wide world of knife sales. And while *that's a brilliant, albeit supervillain-level evil, scheme to work your way up the pyramid* . . . those aren't dates. (Even if you leave the knife presentation and make out in the car. Still not a date.)

(10) Coffee shop. I respect coffee shops. They're great places to talk without leaning on the crutch of alcohol. But I've never had a great coffee shop date because it's a dead end, not a . . . um . . . live beginning. It doesn't lead anywhere. You meet at a coffee shop, have a drink, talk for 90 minutes, and then that's it—no momentum, no burst of energy, no mounting sexual tension. *You end up going home;* you don't pick up and head to the next coffee shop for another latte. No one does coffee shop crawls.

(11) Karaoke. Let's deal with some rough numbers here I've pulled out of midair.[131]

50 percent of people hate karaoke outright—they're scared to do it, they don't know lyrics, etc.

20 percent of people aren't outright mortified by karaoke—but wouldn't want to sing on a date where early impressions are on the line.

10 percent like karaoke too much and use it as a chance to show off a great voice and, regrettably, a vast knowledge of show tunes.

10 percent have bad voices.[132]

---

[131] Anyone who quotes statistics and doesn't admit to just pulling them out of midair is lying. Fourteen percent of all people know that.

[132] And not "cute bad," like a preschool class singing "Eensy Weensy Spider," But "bad bad," like a preschool class being devoured by evil murderous spiders in a horror movie with a title like *Nap Time* or *No Child Left Behind.*

Which leaves about 10 percent of people who have the balls to sing karaoke, the chops to pull it off, the creativity to pick a good song, and the absence of *American Idol* delusions. Odds that both you and your date are part of that 10 percent? Yikes. Let's just keep the "pulling numbers out of thin air" train going and say it's one in three million.

11 First- and Second-Date Conversation Dos and Don'ts

Ideally, your first- and second-date conversations are going to flow so smoothly and naturally that you're both wondering why it took so long for the universe (or, if you're having your first date on *Lost*, the island) to bring you together. In reality, that doesn't always happen. So while you don't want to come off too rehearsed and over-prepared for your first and second dates, keeping a few of these in your head might help you out during one of those DEFCON 1 silences.

(1) DO: Politics. I've never understood why there's such a hard-and-fast "don't talk politics on a first date" rule. Here's how I see it: *If you care enough about politics that they're going to be a major factor in whether or not you're compatible with a person, you do yourself a disservice by being afraid to talk about them.*[133]

And if you aren't knowledgeable about politics, you're governmentally indifferent, or you're a member of some really, really radical party (like the Gay Klansmen for the Status Quo or the New Whigs on the Block), then maybe you shouldn't be arguing politics regardless—whether it's a first date, fiftieth date, or tenth wedding anniversary.

(2) DON'T: Prepackaged top-five lists. If you are going to prepackage a few emergency conversation topics, don't just pull out

---

[133] I have a friend who works for one of the California senators. (Hint: It's the liberal female one.) She was talking to a guy at a bar here in California. He asked about her job. She told him the name of the senator she works for. He said, "Oh yeah, I've heard of her, I think she's actually my senator." They did not go on a date.

a nonsequitur list ("What are your five favorite breakfast cereals?"; "What are your five biggest superstitions?"; "What are your five favorite movie dogs?"; "What are your five favorite Frank Sinatra songs?")

I'd avoid questions like that altogether because *they seem so forced.* But if you *must* do them, at least make them non–nonsequitur ("What are your five favorite breakfast cereals?" "Oh cool, I like Lucky Charms, too! What are your five biggest superstitions?" "Yeah, no one likes cats. What are your five favorite movie dogs?" "Lady and the Tramp *are* the best. What are your five favorite Frank Sinatra songs?").

(3) DO: Talk positively about family—yours and in general. If there's one thing that's a universally recognized red flag—besides the Nazi Germany flag, which is a giant red flag both figuratively and literally—it's having a negative attitude toward family. *Your family, starting a family, anything family related—find a way to give it a positive spin.*

(4) DON'T: One-up stories. By constantly one-upping stories, you're sending the message: *"Everything I've done in my life is slightly to hugely more interesting than everything you've done in yours."* And no matter how true that is, it's still an off-putting message to send.

So if he's telling you a story about the time he got to see Cirque du Soleil in Vegas—and you have a story ready to go about the time you ran away to join the circus but inadvertently joined the French-Canadian circus so you had to tour around Quebec wearing a bright turquoise jester's outfit pulling rainbows out of a top hat—put that in your pocket for a later date.

(5) DO: Vary up the topics. Because it's *very rare that amazing hookups come out of dates that painfully and endlessly stagnate on just one subject.* This sentence does not exist: "So he talked to me about the reasons that Epcot Center is underrated for two straight hours, then we went home and banged."

(6) DON'T: Ask "What else is new?" or "So what else should I know about you?" I hate when people say those phrases, because they're a rare trifecta of bad subtext: (1) The conversation has hit a dead spot, but it's not my fault; (2) I am not clever enough to think on my feet and figure out a new subject to talk about; and (3) I'm perfect, and it's your job to impress me.

These are the biggest panic moves—ennui has set in, the date's on its way to disaster, and you need to say *something*. So you say the first thing you can think of, only it doesn't start a conversation, *it just deflects that responsibility* onto the other person. And no one appreciates a person who passes the buck. We get enough of that in Washington! Am I right? Anyone?

(7) DO: Only lie through omission. If you tell a bunch of lies and he/she believes you, that's fine in the short term. But *what if you guys actually date for a while*?

I ran into trouble with this once. Bored, at a bar, my friend Josh introduced me to a girl as "one of the kids from *Home Alone*." I proceeded to tell her stories about my time on set with Macaulay Culkin, about how I actually came up with the move where he put his hands on his face and yelled, and on and on. She loved it; Josh and I found it hilarious; everybody wins.

The problem was . . . after that, we kinda clicked. About four dates later, she called me out on the *Home Alone* thing and, as much as I tried to smooth talk my way out of it, I really couldn't. I'd booby-trapped the relationship by starting it with lies—you can avoid 'em for a little while but, eventually, you're going to step on the toy cars or get hit in the head by a flying paint can.

(8) DON'T: Talk about prices or tip. Let's break this one up by gender:

For men: Pay for the first two, probably three, dates, no questions asked—even if she was the one who asked you out.[134] Give some hint as to what you're going to order to give the woman a price range to shoot for. Don't order the cheapest bottle of wine . . . but there's no need to order the most expensive one, either.[135] Leave a full 20 percent tip (post-tax) but don't brag about it or not-so-subtly ask your date, "Hey, what's 20 percent of $94?"[136]

For women: Assume he's paying, and find out what he's ordering to get the price range. Don't order the most expensive glass of wine on the menu, but there's no need to order the cheapest one, either. *Offer to pay, expect him to say no, and don't insist*—and if he does take you up on it, immediately take sexual relations off the menu for that night.

(9) DO: Stay positive when you talk about things. Assume that someone's *presenting the idealized version of him/ herself on a date.* So if that trying-to-impress, song-and-dance version includes a nonstop barrage of complaints about rubbery chicken, a crazy boss, the economy, how the fat cats don't care about the little guy, the temperature in here, CBS's fall lineup, overfishing, and how the other gender sucks in every way; imagine what's going to happen when he/she's actually *comfortable* with you.

---

[134] Yep. You've got to do this, as much as it sucks. And when she makes a token gesture to offer to pay or split it, say no. If you say yes, that immediately jumps to the lead when she's describing the date to people the next day. That being said, if she doesn't make a token gesture, then she's spoiled, and you should take that into consideration.

[135] I heard from a friend in the wine business that restaurants know that no one wants to order the cheapest bottle of wine. So the cheapest bottle they list and the second-cheapest bottle they list are probably the same in quality, only they know they're going to sell way more of the second-cheapest one. That's why I recommend ordering the THIRD-cheapest one. You'll drop an extra $5 or so, but the jump in quality is going to be much larger than you think.

[136] She'll somehow find out how much you tipped on her own. She's a woman—they channel their inner Nancy Drew when it comes to sizing up a guy's current (and prospective future) financial situation.

(10) DON'T: Order for the other person. In the 1982 movie *Fast Times at Ridgemont High*, the cool guy is teaching the nerdy guy about dates, and tells him that ordering for the woman is a class move. I don't know. That *feels very antiquated to me.* Like it was cool in *Fast Times*, but now it's just off-putting and unnecessarily presumptuous (coincidentally, just like Sean Penn).

(11) DO: Talk about other dates. People are generally mortified at the thought of discussing previous relationships on a date—and it's generally smart to avoid them. But while you don't want to talk endlessly about how much you miss your ex or how many people currently have restraining orders against you, *there's nothing wrong with talking about BAD dates you've been on.*

If you want to get some insight into his/her dating preferences, see him/her get animated and funny, ask to hear a bad date story.[137]

Word of caution: Don't ask that to break a lull in a conversation. If you've hit a tough pause, you're both scrambling for a topic and the first thing that pops into your mind is "tell me about your other bad dates" . . . think about the message that sends.

---

[137] This conversation topic is tripled for people you meet through online dating. Everyone who does online dating has a ratio of like two bad dates for every good one. You'll have a lifetime's supply of weird date stories in less than a month. And so will the person you're with. So let 'em fly.

11 Things You Should Eat on Your
First 11 Dates

Dating and eating are eternally linked. They're like Harry Potter and Voldemort in that way. In absolutely no way *other* than that, however. It's not the world's most 1:1 metaphor. No wonder the Sorting Hat put me on the remedial track.

(1) First date: Nothing. It's a fairly universal practice now to avoid doing a meal on a first date. I don't think you have to make this the law—if you met someone at a Greek Food Appreciation Symposium,[138] and the main thing you both have in common is a love of Greek food, and some *Top Chef* sixth-runner-up just opened a new Greek restaurant in town, there's no reason to skip it and go to a bar just to follow the rules.

Generally, though, *you're going to want to make a first date a weekday drinks date.* It's low commitment, it's inherently short . . . and if it's going poorly, it's easy to bail. So on the first date, all you should plan on eating is the lime in your drink. If things are going well you can order an appetizer together.

(2) Second date: Tapas, Thai, or sushi. What do these all have in common? They hit the right second-date price point, they're faux-exotic so you look cool, they're good cuisines for drinkin', and they're light, so no feels bloated or nappy afterward.[139]

Also, operating under the assumption that a second date is probably going to lead to some kind of kiss, *none of these has*

---

[138] If such a thing absolutely exists, someone please e-mail me and tell me when it is. If you do, you'll be my gyro baby.

[139] I mean "nappy" as in "wanting a nap" not at *all* in the Don Imus way.

an awful taste that lingers in your mouth and stands strong, impervious to gum or mints.[140]

(3) Third date: Italian. Italian's a real meal. It's a commitment. It's richer food; it's romantic food. *Atmosphere matters.* So lean toward an nicer Italian restaurant—three steps above Olive Garden and two steps above a place where an organ grinder and monkey go table to table trying to get you to sing "That's Amore." (Actually, scratch that. If you guys are meant to be, he/she's going to be the kind of person who appreciates a dancing monkey invading your date.)

(4) Fourth date: Someplace cheaper. No specific cuisine necessary. It's just that on the fourth date, *the female is going to feel compelled to pay.* You know what's even more gentlemanly than paying on the first three dates? *Not* ordering surf and turf—where the menu only says "Seasonal" instead of an actual price[141]—and making her pay for it on the fourth one.

(5) Fifth date: Mexican. I think this is a good fifth date for two reasons. One, margaritas are a legalized version of the *Men in Black* mind-erasing gun, so they can *help get over some awkwardness over potential fifth date physicality.* That's right—it's just about time to get physical.[142] And two, because this is the first date where you could accidentally fart and probably be able to talk your way out of it.[143]

---

[140] In general, I recommend avoiding garlic on dates. If gum and mints are Mario, garlic is Bowser. If gum and mints are Superman, garlic is Lex Luthor. If gum and mints are Van Helsing, garlic is . . . well . . . not Dracula. I've painted myself into a corner. Time to bail.

[141] I was going to reference a scene in the movie *Booty Call* here, because they talk about "Seasonal" pricing on menus, except that would make it like four different *Booty Call* references in this book. Frankly one is too many.

[142] I heard that *Dating for Dummies* recommends waiting three months before you have sex. Talk about not knowing your audience. If there's anyone who's going to be ready and willing to jump into bed early, logical consequences be damned, it's dummies.

[143] In its defense, *Dating for Dummies* does not cover farting on dates.

(6) Sixth date: Home cooking. I operate under the assumption that two good cooks will never date. I do not know why but it always seems like one person in a couple wants to create dishes that incorporate words like "reduction" or "confit" and the other person is all "microwave for 45 seconds, then stir in the powdered cheese."[144]

The sixth date is *a good chance for the one of you that cooks to show off* with a nice, thoughtful dinner at home. Make something with a reduction (or macaroni and cheese that uses Gruyère and is, in no way, easy).

(7) Seventh date: Brunch. Not every meal has to be a dinner, and this is a good point for your first brunch—*either because it follows a sleepover or because you're doing an entire weekend day together.* And you two can really appreciate brunch—while single people, friends, or families *can* eat brunch, true brunch is a couples activity.

(8) Eighth date: Someplace healthy. Eating all these great, rich, delicious meals together is a fantastic experience. Around date eight you are starting to notice some of the effects on your body. So you say, "We've got to eat somewhere healthy," and he/she goes, "YES. Oh my God, yes." So then you go and have salads and *feel like you've really made a difference in your health levels.* Whether you actually have is arguable. Especially if your salads involve the words "tuna," "Chinese," "macaroni," "steak," "ranch," "Southwest," or, worst of all, "taco."

(9) Ninth date: With your friends. The ninth date means *there's some real longevity here.* So it's OK to invite him/her out to a meal with your friends.

---

[144] However, it is possible for two bad cooks to date. It keeps the restaurant industry alive. Leftover shrimp fried rice is a totally viable breakfast food.

For instance, on many a Sunday morning, my friends and I go to breakfast. I would call it brunch but, as I mentioned before, that's a couples activity, and also, brunch sounds classy—and we usually just have a sloppy orgy of food where everyone in a three-foot radius is probably getting splashed with gravy or Thousand Island.

After nine dates, I'd absolutely feel comfortable bringing someone into that world. It might end up happening a little earlier circumstantially, but that's risky. Once you open someone's eyes to you participating in a food orgy, unless he/she is already totally sold on you, you'll probably ruin your chances of participating in a real orgy together.

(10) Tenth date: A place you already went. Ten dates in, you've started really figuring out what you both like. And you can stop doing the *It's a Small World* tour of restaurants and focus in on a place you both loved.

Repeating a restaurant is a big signal of your comfort level in the relationship. It's nice when you can relax and stop feeling like everything you say and do has to be brilliant. Of course, that means the initial magical spark is fading . . . so it's also a point where a lot of people completely lose interest. But hey, if that's the case, at least you're eating your last meal together somewhere you both really like.

(11) Eleventh date: Ribs . . . maybe. You can't do ribs any earlier than this. That also goes for Buffalo wings, chili cheeseburgers, buffets, or the steakhouse from *The Great Outdoors*. *Save the messy foods and eating contests for down the road,* when spotting barbecue sauce on the inside of each other's nostrils— or eating four pounds of steak in 45 minutes to win a T-shirt—isn't a potential relationship killer.

11 Red Flags in Your Home That Will Scare Off Women

Inside every woman there's a miniature health inspector, just waiting with a clipboard and red pen, ready to give your place a subatomic evaluation. And if you fail, unlike a condemned restaurant, you probably won't get a chance for a second evaluation once you scrub your cutting boards more thoroughly and tweak your refrigerator temperature.

(1) Messy bathroom. There is nothing that makes or breaks your apartment like the cleanliness of the bathroom. Nothing. Just remember: when she's deciding whether or not to let you drip sweat all over her naked body,[145] she has to picture the environment where she'll clean up afterward. And if there's a moldy shower curtain, a rusty drain, an empty roll of toilet paper, a dirty toilet, and a shaggy bath mat that looks like it could be a petri dish playing host to the genesis of a new species of bacteria, she won't want to be naked there.[146]

Conversely, if you invest in a nice bathroom, it can actually make her *more* likely to want to have sex because she actually *wants* to clean up in there. Remember that: ***Bathrooms are a brilliant investment.*** They're better investments than soy, Chick-Fil-A

---

[145] Or, if you're on network TV or basic cable, her body with a bra on and your lower halves covered by a sheet.

[146] In college, when I was living with three friends, the area behind the radiator in our bathroom was so filthy that one time I dropped a bar of soap back there and found it to be un-cleanable. Soap. Our bathroom made soap un-cleanable. That's not how you cultivate a fun, sexy vibe. Or even a basic-standard-of-living vibe.

franchises, or a mint condition collection of rare toys, figurines, and miniatures.

(2) A mint condition collection of rare toys, figurines, or miniatures. My friend Carrie once went on a decent date with a guy. When she went back to the guy's place, in his dining room was an expensive oaken glass case containing tons of cheeky porcelain miniatures. She made an excuse and left. And every single time I've told another woman that story, she agreed wholeheartedly with that decision.

So if you have a collection of toys, or miniatures, or figurines, or dolls, or anything that would be collected by a 73-year-old grandma, Ned Flanders, or Steve Carell in The *40-Year-Old Virgin*, keep them under wraps for a while. Just *tell yourself it's helping to preserve their value.* (They *are* almost as good of a long-term investment as a nice bathroom, after all.)

(3) Deep video game passion. Video games have come a long, long way. They're completely mainstream. Women even play them—maybe not *Fallout 3*, but definitely *Wii Sports*. But if there's *evidence that you take your gaming to the next level,* that could make her raise an eyebrow. Having tattered strategy guides or an industrial-strength racing wheel or a Rock Band drum kit that's larger and more expensive than a real drum kit—these are all signs that your free time is going to be split between her and yelling at racist 14-year-olds on Xbox Live.

(4) Suspicious photos. Men can overlook photos pretty easily. We know women love putting up photos. The reverse isn't always true. *When a guy puts up a photo, generally it's because he's been coerced to* or because it really, really means something to him.

A woman will intensely Zapruder the photos you have on your walls looking for any evidence of your deep, dark secrets. So beware of photos that cast huge suspicion: lots of photos that seem to be with the same woman; no photos with male friends; a photo of your grandmother in a spot that's visible from bed; a photo of you posing at Disneyland with your secret second family; or a photo of your kid whom you haven't ever mentioned to her.[147]

(5) Evidence of another woman. Women are always *on high alert for signs of competition.* If there's a tampon wrapper in your bathroom garbage, she'll notice. If you have a few pieces of women's clothing in your closet—and you don't sing "Proud Mary" in drag shows—she'll spot them. If there are long hairs on the sheets or pillow, she'll find them.[148]

(6) Furniture that was acceptable in college but not now. In college, anything goes. Build a coffee table out of a stolen stop sign and two cinder blocks? Let's do it. Poster of Belushi in *Animal House* wearing a sweatshirt that says "College"? Scotch-tape that shit to the wall. See a soiled couch on the side of the road? Throw the two homeless people masturbating off it and grab a side! Sleep on a futon? Hell, let's *all* sleep on futons.

This *loses its charm approximately four seconds after you graduate* (or drop out). Now your furniture should match—even if that just means buying everything at IKEA that's the same shade of particleboard. Your coffee table should be an actual table. Your posters should be in frames (and referencing things other than college and beer). And you should sleep on a bed, with a frame—not just a mattress on the ground, and especially not a futon. Adult women don't want to have sex on transformable furniture.

(7) A barren refrigerator. So your fridge has the following contents: 18 beers, mustard, half of a leftover order of carne asada,

---

[147] It varies from woman to woman whether she'll date a guy with a kid. But *no* woman is going to want to date a guy who has a kid but ignores him.

[148] Yes, the woman you're dating is a regular She-lock Holmes. No, that entire paragraph wasn't a setup for that pun.

a stick of margarine, and a box of wine.[149] That's fine for you—you don't cook, and you shouldn't have to. (Frankly, some women like the fact that you don't cook because it means you'll never be able to let her go since she can.)

But, early on, your barren refrigerator is a red flag. *Women take their eating schedules extremely seriously.* Much more seriously than men, strangely enough. They're like lions at the zoo. If they don't get their food when they want it, someone's getting mauled. So if she's at your house and it's feeding time, she's not going to be satisfied with a beer and mustard.

(8) Lots of roommates. I've spent much of my adult life living with three male roommates. At some point, every girl I dated eventually used the term "frat house" in a pejorative way.[150]

Anyway, I was generally able to overcome living in a "frat house" and have success—but I will say that *I leaned against bringing girls there early on.* I was afraid—and, I think, rightfully so—that I would lose them on the spot once they saw my state of arrested development.[151]

(9) A lot of drug paraphernalia. Having one pipe or regular-sized bong in the closet doesn't indicate a problem. But you *leave the realm of "having a good time" for "8 to 10 years in prison"* when you have a greenhouse out back containing an entire field of poppies; a bunch of spoons with burn marks on the bottoms; or a collection of hypodermic needles even though you're not a doctor, diabetic, or traveling needle salesman.

(10) Unwashed sheets. I'd estimate that the average single male washes his bedsheets about one-10th as often as the average

---

[149] Literally a dozen of my friends just read that line and thought I was describing their fridges.
[150] It's like they get hit in the head with one flying keg, and all of a sudden things need to change or something.
[151] Yep. I'm a Bluth. At least I know there's always money in the banana stand.

single female. And yes, *that means that the sheets don't get washed every time after sexual relations.*

So if your sheets don't look crisp and tight, as freshly washed sheets should, the first thought in her mind is going to be, "If CSI ran a black light over those things, would they look tie-dyed?"[152] And then that mental image is going to flat-out repulse her.

(11) ***The Game*** **or other pickup strategy books.** However, in a random poll I conducted, 100 percent of women say that having a copy of *this* 11 Points book would be a huge turn-on. So *buy this book for all of your friends and keep it out on the coffee table* (which, naturally, is the same matching particleboard color as the rest of the furniture in your living room).

---

[152] And her second thought will be: "I shouldn't be able to do a thread count on one hand."

11 Red Flags in Your Home That Will
Scare Off Men

I'm going to leave off super-intuitive stuff like "a wedding dress," "a pink razor on the ledge of the bathtub that's jammed full with curly copper-colored hairs," and "a chocolate-colored sex toy on the nightstand that's the size of a can of Pringles."[153]

(1) The wrong number of cats. I don't think cats are necessarily the turnoff that *Last Comic Standing* contestants think they are.

If you have one cat, you're not a spinster. Your cat won't exactly be a guy magnet—a dog who runs up and excitedly jumps at a guy is going to do more for your stock in four seconds than a cat would do in 30 years—but the cat isn't going to completely sink you.

You might even be able to get away with two cats, if you're witty and at least one of the cats doesn't have the traditional "I'm a standoffish asshole" cat personality. Anything more, though, and when the guy and his friends are coming up with their nickname for you, there are going to be a lot of suggestions that include the phrase "crazy cat lady."

(2) A huge, visible tampon collection. By huge, *I'm referring to the number of visible tampons, not the width or absorbency of said tampons.*

(3) Cheap bedsheets. One of the best things about sleeping at a woman's place—besides, you know, the sex stuff—are the sheets. Women are far more likely to invest in high thread counts, plush

---

[153] On that note, what's the deal with Pringles coming in the same cans as tennis balls? I don't know whether to eat the chips or *serve* them.

duvet covers, and expensive pillows. And the sheets are freshly washed and smell great.[154]

All of this means: *If you have bad sheets, he's going to be extremely disappointed.* No, it won't be enough to keep him from undulating all over you . . . but when he's trying to picture himself spending hundreds of future nights in that bed, irresistible sheets are really going to help grease the wheels on that vision.

(4) A streaked toilet. Much like men try to pretend that tampons don't exist, we try doubly hard to believe women don't pulverize the toilet, either.[155] A guy won't examine a bathroom for cleanliness as aggressively as a woman does. He won't notice soap scum or a clogged drain. But *he will notice, and be quickly turned off by, a befouled toilet.* It suspends his suspension of disbelief.

(5) *Sex and the City* DVDs. This is nothing against *Sex and the City*—sure, some people say the movies are offensively condescending toward women and/or filmmaking, but the TV show actually had some good moments. And puns. So many awesome puns.

The reason *SatC* is a red flag is because every guy has, at some point, been burned by a woman who formulated some fantasy or dating theory or belief out of something that she saw on the show. *Men genuinely believe that* SatC *poisons women.* So seeing that you're a hard-core fan just makes him positive you're going to pull some kind of ridiculous gambit sooner or later that will probably ruin or, at least, severely fracture your relationship.

Maybe this whole point is overly pessimistic of me but, ya know, I'm a Miranda.

---

[154] You run a CSI black light over those things and you know what you'd see? Nothing. Just specks of dust. Not a single fluid in sight. It's beautiful.

[155] I had a female coworker once who said she and her cohabitating boyfriend decided that when she would go into the bathroom for extended periods of time it was to "drizzle honey." I like that.

(6) Labeled cabinets, toothpaste rollers, and other signs of deep neuroses. I've dated two women who've had this device on their toothpaste tube. It's a little plastic clip that you put at the end that keeps it tightened and flattened as you squeeze out toothpaste, ensuring none is wasted.

This tool is, to me, the ultimate sign of cartoon bad guy/Howard Hughes–style neuroses. Anyone who's willing to buy a toothpaste clip (and then religiously use it) probably has your relationship planned out on a calendar.[156]

It also means that, unless you're obsessive-compulsive, *your house will never be organized enough for her to be comfortable* there. And incongruous standards on organization and cleanliness tank an exceptionally high number of relationships.

(7) Tons of really expensive shoes. Men don't know shoe brands very well. Louboutin sounds to us like a shorthand nickname for Louis Vuitton and we think Manolo Blahnik was the star of *Blossom*. But we do know when shoes look expensive, and we do know that expensive women's shoes cost more than Korean cars.

So when we see a closet dedicated to shoes or expensive ones being put on display, all we think of is *how many organs we'd have to sell on the black market to buy you even one more pair.* Obsessing about designer shoes is a *much* more expensive kind of foot fetish than the traditional male foot fetish, by the way.

(8) An old TV. Men tend to invest far more into electronics than women. We absolutely refuse to spend $50 on matching towels, but we'll gladly spend 40 times that to have a giant TV that's way too big for the living room.

It's not that we'd expect you to have a top-of-the-line big screen. But we'd like to think that, perhaps, *if things work out between us, you'd be amenable to spending money on that kind of*

---

[156] However, if you like the rhythm method, a woman like that is a godsend.

setup. And if you have a TV that needs one of those government-subsidized converter boxes because it came with rabbit ears[157] or a GE-brand 17-inch one that you've clearly been lugging around since your freshman-year dorm room—as dumb as this sounds, it can actually hurt our thoughts on our long-term relationship prospects.

And short-term, it'll make us reluctant to watch romantic comedies with you at your house. I don't want to watch them on a tiny, standard definition TV where I have to squint to see Renée Zellweger.

(9) More than two instances of motivational quotes on the walls. Women seem to really love posters and artwork that contains motivational quotes: "Dare to dream"; "One smile can change the world"; "Shoot for the moon, and if you miss you'll land in the stars."[158]

Having a few of these is normal. It won't register in the guy's head. But if you've blanketed your place in motivational posters, suddenly he's going to believe you're hiding issues—*deep, debilitating self-esteem issues.* No one needs *that* many posters. There are only so many cats that can tell you to "Hang in there, baby" before you either *do* start hanging in there or give up entirely.

Also, if you're a *The Secret* type, go ahead and toss that vision board in the closet, too. I don't want to know the man you're really visualizing for yourself is Matt Lauer, and I'm some low-rent substitute.

---

[157] For people reading this in the future, once upon a time the government decided to give people money so they could buy a box that would convert their old-fashioned TVs into bottom-of-the-line new-fashioned TVs. Just in case you're wondering why your generation inherited a $5 quintillion deficit.

[158] Even though the basic science behind that quote is completely flawed—the moon is way closer to Earth than any stars. You should aim for the stars so if you miss you'll land and hit the moon.

(10) A male roommate who's clearly in love with you (a.k.a. any male roommate). *If you have a male roommate, we will believe he is in love with you.* And since he has home-court advantage, we will believe he's going to do whatever it takes to stand in our way—and ultimately win out.

Unless he's in a relationship, gay, or still-in-the-closet-but-clearly gay, there's nothing you can say that will make us believe your roommate isn't secretly in love with you. So I'm not saying you should ditch your roommate because he's a guy, and that's going to hurt your dating life . . . but I'm saying you should at least consider it.

(11) A sink full of dishes. Yes, it's a chauvinistic, antiquated double standard. But one of the top reasons men look forward to getting married is having someone to take a lead on washing dishes. (Or, for a lot of us, actually purchasing nonpaper dishes.) So if you think he's maybe, just maybe, sizing you up as a potential wife, *he's going to keep an eye on all of those old-fashioned domestic tasks.* So all those unwashed dishes just stagnating there will . . . wait for it . . . sink you. That pun's for you, Carrie Bradshaw.

11-Step Checklist to Get Ready for a Date

This is based off of a checklist I actually made for myself to get ready for dates. I even wrote it down once. Then I panicked about what would happen if a girl found it, so I tore it up into pieces and threw them into two separate garbage cans. Apparently I thought she'd be so curious to see my pre-date agenda that she'd go through my trash and tape my list back together. I'm kind of a lost cause sometimes.

(1) Cleaning: 2+ hours before date. If you're the one driving, your car should be washed and cleaned inside. Front *and* back seats. The fast food soda cup collection, stockpile of gas receipts, changes of clothes, tennis rackets—all gotta go. *This goes double if you plan on hooking up in the backseat;* when you throw down the condom wrapper, it shouldn't hit a Whopper wrapper.

If you think there's a chance this date could end up back at your place—even a remote, remote chance—you need to clean it up, too. Even if you live with roommates and they're the ones who made the mess. Go bathroom first, area where you'll be hanging out second, bedroom third.

(2) Grooming: 1.5–2 hours before date. Take a few steps to look your best. That means tooth brushing, shaving, and de-unibrowing. And remember: if you might end up in a seminude state a few hours later, you need to groom the rest of your person, too.[159]

---

[159] Interesting reversal on that too: I had a friend who didn't "trust [her]self" on dates, so she wouldn't shave her legs or wear attractive underwear on purpose. Because she knew no matter what, she wouldn't let a guy down there with everything in that state of disrepair.

Addendum for women: When it comes to makeup, I've found that guys seem to prefer less to more. While some is good, you want to avoid drifting into "orange clown" territory. You'll bring his childhood fear of clowns storming back. (And if he had a childhood fear of oranges, that, too.)

Addendum for men: If you only have 30 seconds to get ready for a date, *spend it on your nails.* Make sure there's no dirt underneath them and that they're neatly trimmed. When a woman sees long nails on a guy, the first and only thought she has is, "I'm not letting those nails touch any part of my body, let alone the mid-southern region."

(3) Clothing: 1 hour before date. What you wear should accomplish two very basic things: You should look good and feel comfortable. That means: *Wear something flattering and attractive that you won't find yourself tugging on all night long* and doesn't require you to wear a Spanx bodysuit underneath.[160]

I also recommend focusing your clothing search on something you wear regularly. For some reason, date-induced mania always seems to lead to grabbing things from the dark recesses of your closet.

(4) Advance notice text: 45 minutes before date. While you're getting dressed, shoot over a quick text like, "Still good to go for 8?" It's *a nice courtesy,* lets the other person get an extension if necessary, and, most important, if he/she uses that last opportunity to flake on you, you can immediately start making new plans. Might as well—you've cleaned up, you're dressed up, and now you're kinda pissed. That's the perfect time to meet your friends out and do some damage.

---

[160] Should I do an obscure *St. Elmo's Fire* reference here? Don't really have the energy. I've got to get back to the caps tournament.

(5) Mint/gum double check: 40 minutes before date.
Aim for a Colgate Cavity Patrol–level of fresh-breath obsessiveness. I've found that, at the end of the date, when the kissing may or may not begin, fresh breath can make him/her forget any and all gaffes you made earlier in the night.

(6) Make a quick contingency plan: 30 minutes before date. I used to always take my dates to this tapas place that was a few blocks from my house. It was perfect. Then one night, a girl and I arrived there and found out it had burned down. (There was some buzz that it might've been arson, although that was the scoop from the drifter outside. The Liberal Media[161] reported that it was a grease fire. I'm still torn on whom to believe.)

I didn't have a contingency plan, and the only alternative that popped into my head was this mediocre Thai place in the neighborhood. And when we went there, believe it or not, it was mediocre.[162]

Take two minutes to grab a reservation at an alternate place nearby—or, at least have an alternate place in mind. Then *you can avoid the whole "uh . . . I don't know where we should go now, what do you think?" debacle.*

(7) Eat something: 20 minutes before date. You should never go to a date starving. If it's a dinner date, *have a snack to take the edge off.* If you're just going for drinks and you *might* order appetizers, basically eat a meal.

---

[161] It gives me some kind of weird joy to use the phrase "Liberal Media." I went to journalism school and really don't remember a single moment of them indoctrinating us with liberal propaganda. Our classes didn't have names like Intro to Editing and Tree-hugging, or Syntax and Spend.

[162] This is a different Thai restaurant than the one mentioned in the introduction to this chapter. No, I never had particularly good luck with Thai restaurants and dates. That's why eventually I said, "(Pad) See You Later" to Thai restaurant dates. Not a lame enough pun? OK, trying again. That's why eventually I said, "Phuket, I'm not taking dates to Thai anymore."

Let's enter an extended metaphor where your body's a ship and it has three different captains that take turns steering: your brain, your stomach, and your loins. On a date, you want the brain or the loins doing the steering, never the stomach. It's going to steer you right into an iceberg (like the RMS *Titanic*, not like "you're going to end up gorging on lettuce").

(8) Temper expectations: 8 minutes before date. Once you're almost ready to go, stand in front of the mirror, look deep into your own eyes, take a deep breath, and say, *"This date is probably going to be awful."*

I'm a big fan of anti-pep talks before dates—not to hurt your confidence, but to relax. Remind yourself: I'm probably not about to go out with my future spouse, probably not even my future boy/girlfriend, and I probably won't end up having sex tonight. I'm just going out to have a good time. No expectations. No pressure.

(9) Ringer off: 2 minutes before date. Cell phones have no place on dates (other than emergencies like, say, your house or mom is on fire). It's just rude to use one. Your date sits there looking like a goon while you talk or text—and has irrefutable proof that you're not putting 100 percent effort and attention into the date.

I know that if *I put my phone on vibrate, it's going to drive me crazy* when it sits there buzzing in my pocket all night. Too tempting. So I turn the ring and vibration off completely. (And when I go to the bathroom, *then* I can tear it out of my pocket and go, "Oh my God what have I missed? Come to me, beloved e-mails! Preview of this week's deals at Staples. Sweeeeeet.")

(10) Four last-second checks: 1 minute before date. Go into the bathroom and make sure of the following things: Sweat wiped from palms . . . *nothing in your teeth* . . . unsightly stray facial/eyebrow hairs gone . . . zipper is up. You can even remember those with the mnemonic "SNUZ." It doesn't mean anything but at least it'll jog your memory better than "HOMES" for the Great Lakes or "MVEMJSUN" for the planets.[163]

(11) Get ready with a compliment: 20 seconds before date. *The only right way to start a date with a woman is to compliment how she looks.* Anything other than that, and you've started off on the wrong foot. She took a lot of time and a lot of effort to get ready. Tell her how good she looks—even if you're lying.[164]

Homer Simpson once said, "When it comes to compliments, women are ravenous, blood-sucking monsters always wanting more, more, more! And if you give it to them, you'll get plenty back in return." And I think he knows a little something. He's ostensibly one of the least sexually appealing men ever, yet over the course of *The Simpsons* no fewer than six attractive women have tried to steal him away from Marge.[165]

---

[163] Notice how I adapted the iconic *Saved by the Bell* MVEMJSUNP there because Pluto's not a planet anymore.

[164] Plus, in the process, you very subtly let her know you're aware of her body, which plants a seed of sexual tension.

[165] Princess Kashmir, Mindy Simmons, Lurleen Lumpkin, Amber in Vegas, Otto's ex Becky, and Julia the opera fan. And Brad the gay guy, too. (I guess Amber's not that attractive. The others are clearly hot.)

11 Keys to Dating
Multiple People at Once

Dating seems to go in cycles. Sometimes you find you have a full roster of prospects who can't get enough of you; sometimes you find yourself mindlessly doodling the words "die alone" on a Post-it at work. This list is for those times when your cup (and daytime minute usage) runneth over—when you have plenty of potential dates and you want to take a shot with all of them.

Important note before jumping in: this list isn't a guide to cheating; it's designed for people dating multiple people on the up-and-up (when you're not in an exclusive relationship—including marriage—and everyone involved understands that you're all technically free to date whomever you want).

(1) Check your conscience (and free time) at the door. Dating multiple people simultaneously is not for rookies. It's like juggling . . . except instead of brightly colored balls you're tossing around other people's emotions, hopes, and sexual activity. I've seen a guy juggle flaming knives, and frankly that seems less precarious.

Before you start dating multiple people simultaneously, you have to recognize a few things: (1) *You're probably going to hurt some feelings;* (2) you're going to have to tell some lies (or, at least, omit some truths);[166] (3) you're going to be making a huge investment of time and money; and (4) if you hate breakup conversations—and, unless you're some kind of freakish sadist, you ought

---

[166] One of my absolute favorite uses of semantics is the difference between lying and omitting truths. It's up there with trying to get out of an argument without actually apologizing for what you did by saying, "I'm sorry that you're upset."

to hate breakup conversations—you may end up having more of them than you've ever had before in your life.

(2) Keep your stories, jokes, anecdotes, and conversations straight. I have a friend who even went as far as *taking notes at the end of his dates* about what was discussed to make sure he could keep things straight. That's an extreme—dating shouldn't require you keeping a court reporter on retainer—but it's illustrative of how carefully you may want to monitor your conversations.

A few times, you can get away with repeating a joke or story: "I told you that already? Are you serious? Man, my memory's going bad with old age." But when it becomes a chronic thing, your dates won't be fun for him/her or for you.

(3) Don't tell the people you're dating about each other. Ever. Philosophies widely vary on this. My opinion: They don't need to know about each other. They know the possibility exists that you're dating other people. They may or may not suspect you are. But when you're with each individual person, as long as you *focus on him/her, give your full effort, and make sure he/she feels special,* then you've handled things correctly.

By talking about the other people you're dating, you're suggesting that *you* have options . . . so the other person should work twice as hard to "win" you. That's not a healthy dating atmosphere.[167]

(4) Don't ask the people you're dating if *they're* dating multiple people. Call it a professional courtesy. Employ a strong "Don't ask, don't tell" policy—those always seem to work smoothly

---

[167] Whenever I can, I like to put things in Backstreet Boys terms, and this is definitely an opportunity. You don't want to cultivate an environment where everyone's saying "Quit Playing Games (With My Heart)"; instead, make sure each one gets "All [You] Have to Give" and knows that, eventually, someone has to be "The One" or you're going to be "Show[n] the Meaning of Being Lonely." That last title was "Incomplete," but I needed to cut it to fit the grammar of the sentence. "I Wanted to Do It That Way."

and without any controversy. But really, *you don't want to be asked, and you shouldn't ask.* Just go ahead and sweep the whole concept of dating multiple people under the rug. Good relationships are built on repressing things.

(5) Only have sex with one person. Ever seen one of those *Maury* episodes where the woman needs 16 different paternity tests to figure out her baby's father? *Don't be that woman. Or one of those guys.* There's something so comically tragic about breaking out into a spontaneous, ecstatic dance routine on national TV because you just found out one of your girlfriend's 15 *other* simultaneous sexual partners fathered the kid you really don't want to be paying for.

(6) Drastically reduce your online presence. It's time to *go off the grid a little bit.* As discussed in the "11 Ways Modern Technology Can Ruin Your Dating Life" list, you're only *one* Facebook photo tag, Twitter reply, or MySpace glittery "Thanks for the hump" wall graphic away from having your entire dating house of cards collapse.

(7) Don't involve your coworkers. I made this mistake. Back when I was dating (and, ya know, back when I had a job) I'd walk into work every morning, and a gaggle of coworkers would ask for my tales of juggling. I would always oblige. Eventually, I started realizing that, as much as they liked the stories, *knowing me only in the context of either working or whoring around made them all form pretty negative opinions of me*—negative opinions that eventually manifested into some actual problems with our ability to work together.

Your coworkers are perfect for conversations about the following edgy topics only: why your boss is a pain in the ass; the finer points of taking office supplies home; who did or didn't have Botox; and why the vending machine guy would make that promise to switch granola bar brands if he wasn't going to pull the trigger. They really don't need to know about your promiscuity—emotional, physical, or both.

(8) Don't try to see everyone all the time (or it will become a job). When your roster gets filled, you very well may find yourself having something scheduled almost every night of the week. On top of that, you'll find yourself in a cycle of nonstop texting and phone calling. Suddenly, your dating life has replaced all of your hobbies and most of your sleep. (You may also find you're drinking five nights a week, never going to the gym, and—this happened to me with *Juno*—seeing the same movie with three different people.)[168]

Pace yourself. *You're just dating these people, not trying to process serve them;* you don't need to either see or heavily correspond with each of them every day. Plus, if you don't, you just increase your mystique. Mystique building through sheer dating exhaustion—that's win-win! (At least for you. It's probably pretty frustrating for them).

(9) Don't cut things off prematurely. This period is fleeting and unsustainable. It's like a pledge to work out every day at 5 AM. You can sustain it for a while, get yourself a little sweaty, but, eventually, you'll be back to a simpler, lazier life.

So, while you're dating multiple people, *don't look at it as a race against the clock to pick one of your prospects and settle down.* Enjoy the process, enjoy the attention, enjoy the ego boost that comes from knowing you finally possess empirical evidence that you're desirable, and let it run its course. Things will naturally sort themselves out when it's time.

(10) Have an endgame in mind. All that being said, you have to have some kind of plan. If you date someone for a few months,

---

[168] Yes, I saw *Juno* three times on three dates with three different girls. Each time I pretended I'd never seen it before. Each time I laughed where I was supposed to laugh, gasped where I was supposed to gasp, and cringed at the phrase "Honest to blog."

he/she's going to find a way to get you into a Define the Relationship talk.[169] So know what you want to get out of this. Do you absolutely want to pick one of the people you're with and have an exclusive relationship, or are you just trying to date everyone in the world without any end in the foreseeable future? Whatever it is, figure out what you're going to do when, out of nowhere, *the people you're dating start coming to cash in their metaphorical chips.*

(11) If you get caught in a sitcom moment, don't try to talk your way out of it. With any luck, you won't have that scenario where you walk into your house and the two girls you're dating are sitting on your couch talking to each other. Or where you're out to dinner with a guy and another guy you're dating walks up and says, "So *this* is your sick grandmother you had to cancel on me for?"

But if it does happen, just recognize that you're busted, apologize to the person you like *less*, and, later, *pull out every piece of charm you've got to salvage things with the one you like more.* It's definitely doable. It's not doable if you try to handle the confrontation like a sitcom character, making up lies, hiding under the table, saying catchphrases like "Check please!" and such.

---

[169] See the "11 Translations of Things Women Say" for a big one of these. "My friends have been asking 'So what are you guys?' And I said, 'I hadn't really thought about it.' But now that they mention it, what *are* we?"

4

SEX

In 1992, I prayed to God for pubic hair.

I was at overnight summer camp. It was the second day, and the first time that all of the boys went to take a shower. We were all 12 or 13 years old, just having finished seventh grade. Everyone stripped down. Out of the corner of my eye I took a look—not motivated by any homosexual curiosity, but rather for invaluable acquisition of knowledge. I wanted to see if they had pubes.

And they did. All of them. Even the ones who were short like me. I did not. I was a late bloomer. Monumentally late. So I decided I was going to do the only thing I could do to avoid a summer of unbearable mockery, and shower in my bathing suit. How I would clean my undercarriage was infinitely less important to me than keeping my hairless secret concealed beneath baggy neon yellow swim trunks.

Anyway, it was a Jewish summer camp (Jews always seem to end up going to their own summer camps) and that meant going to services on Friday night and Saturday morning. That first weekend, I stood there, during a silent Jewish prayer and I reached out to God—inadvertently doing a grotesque bastardization of "Are You There God, It's Me, Margaret?"

"God," I said, "I need only one thing from you. Please, please, please let me grow pubes." I don't remember what I promised to do in return, but I'm sure I tried to broker a good deal. (It's a Jewish thing. You wouldn't understand.) And every service, all summer long, I said the same prayer. The prayer for pubic hair.[170]

Well . . . God clearly de-prioritized my prayer (the early nineties must've been busy for him). I remained hairless for that summer (and showered all summer in a bathing suit). And for all of eighth grade. And for the summer after eighth grade. And for ninth grade. Finally, in the summer after ninth grade, I spotted my first pubic hair. I had just turned 15 years old. I bloomed *that* late.

Jump ahead 10 years. I'm 25, living in Los Angeles, and dating a woman almost 11 years older than I. But, more important, she was the first person I'd dated who had the sexual experience and confidence to correct my many, many, many horrible flaws and habits.

"Sam," she told me one night, "you need to take care of yourself down there. I've never seen a guy with that much pubic hair."

Somewhere deep down, that hairless 12-year-old boy smiled. But on the surface, the 25-year-old—well, I'm reluctant to say "man" so let's go with "fella"—faced a legitimate dilemma. I mean, I had prayed for those pubic hairs. Prayed. And I knew they were long. I was proud they were long! Could I really bring myself to shave them off, even some of them, when they served as a daily reminder of how far I'd come? Instead of being like Tupac and getting a tattoo to remind me of The Struggle, I had pubes. Lots and lots of pubes.

At this point in the book I'd like to pause for a moment and give a quick hello to my parents, grandma, family members, and parents' friends. How's everyone doing? Can't wait to see you all again next time I'm in town! Now back to the story.

---

[170] For some reason, I suspect there won't be a line of rabbis at my door asking me for more info so they can add this to the prayer books.

Ultimately, grooming won out. I bought a trimmer at Bed Bath & Beyond—after making a huge scene about how I was looking for a nose-hair trimmer, because I was embarrassed to reveal the actual motivation—and macheted through a decade of tangles.

Grooming has to win out. It's part of the deal. If you want to be a good sexual partner—if you want to be intimate with someone more than once—you have to grow, change, adapt, and improve. This chapter focuses on all of those. Because even if you're sure you're a master of the sexual arts who's perfect in every way, there's always a little room to evolve.

And if you really refuse to grow, or change, or adapt then, well . . . I guess I'll keep you in my prayers. (Bumping out the current things I pray for, like, fittingly, *less* random body hair.)

11 Sex Tricks and Techniques
Women Will Absolutely Love

I was at a used bookstore a few years back and saw an old book called *The Female Orgasm*. It was at least 300 pages long, with, I assume, only minimal pictures. (And they'd be those black-and-white line-art illustrations that somehow make the vulva look like it's the subject of a *Wall Street Journal* feature.)

The point I'm meandering toward: women are sexually complicated. The things that work great with one won't work quite right with another. My goal for this list was just to get as close as possible to pinning down some near-universal female wants and needs. Consider it the abridged version of *The Female Orgasm*.

(1) Take control. Every woman who somehow found herself in bed with me—usually charmed by some mixture of dumb jokes and geographical convenience—wanted me to take control. Even the ones who were much taller (and, gulp, the one who was much stronger) than I. It's just *one of those gender-role things that hasn't gone away because no one really wants it to.*

(If you do want to switch it up, though, there are an infinite selection of dominatrixes and submissives hanging out online. Craigslist has really been a boon to that industry. It's like what eBay did for people who love really old teapots.)

(2) Decelerate. Squared. If you were to give women a survey to fill out after you hook up with them—and, by the way, if you actually did this, it would be absolutely incredible and bring a whole new meaning to the concept of Yelping—almost all of them would say you jetted through things too quickly. In two ways.

You plowed through foreplay like you had a plane to catch, and when you did stop to perform any kind of action, you plowed through that, too, like you had a . . . did I already say plane to catch? Shit. Let's go with that again.

The best way to turn on a man is to dive right in for his genitals. The best way to turn on a woman is to focus on every area *except* her genitals (at least for a while). So slow down in two ways: both in *how long you wait before escalating things, and in how long you spend on each of those things.* Warm up the engine before you ignite the thrusters and go full throttle.[171]

(3) Be gentle on the gentle parts. I have very rough hands.[172] So when I touched my first breast (by that I mean the first breast on a female, not my own first breast), I squeezed it like I was trying to turn it into a diamond. The girl made a face. And not the face of ecstasy.

That was my first lesson in being gentle. My subsequent lessons would come from almost every other woman I'd be with in the future, each of whom would, at some point, comment on how I was handling a woman's body, not a rack of lamb.

The lesson learned: Basically, *any part of a woman you need special permission to touch requires you to be gentle* (that includes her breasts, anything in her genital region and, as Melanie Griffith said in *Milk Money*, her heart).[173]

---

[171] Full disclosure: I'm writing this at Cleveland Hopkins International Airport right now while I wait for my flight back to L.A., and I may or may not be slightly distracted by all the shiny planes out the window.

[172] The worst I ever did in any class in my entire schooling life was eighth-grade art class, when I manhandled every attempt at pottery and ended up not being able to make even a single non-deformed bowl.

[173] I love ruining a good sex conversation by bringing up that moment in *Milk Money.* I highly recommend it. Next time you're with friends and everyone's trading sex stories and tips, say, "You know where you can touch a woman to really make her go crazy?" And when they all lean in hoping to get some insight into the back of the knee or the right earlobe or the elbow, hit them with, "Her heart." Totally ruins the vibe.

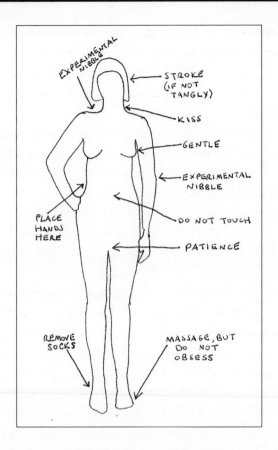

(4) Be a little rough on the rougher parts. This goes back to the "take control" point. Often, adding *the slightest element of Cro-Magnon roughness seems to trigger something primal* in a woman. By that, of course, I don't mean the whole clubbing and dragging her to a cave thing—I mean that you should focus on positioning her where you want her, holding her waist, things of that ilk.[174]

---

[174] If you want to establish a safe word, well, go for it. I'm not really talking about being *that* rough, but if she wants to really escalate things, it's a good idea to choose one. Just don't make your safe word "yes" or "more."

(5) Appreciate her underwear and grooming. Women work hard on underwear. I first learned this during *10 Things I Hate About You*, where the girl who wasn't Julia Stiles held up a pair of black underwear and said, "A girl buys black underwear for someone to see."[175]

She spent good money on that underwear, so *admire it before you take it off* of her. Trust me, if she switches to her less sexy underwear, you'll hate it. I'd even go as far as to say it would be one of some number of things you hate about her.

(6) Keep yourself groomed. You *don't have to go completely hairless* (although it will make your stuff look enormous—bigger than it's looked in years). But you want to significantly trim; even if, as a young boy, you prayed to God for your pubic hair.

(7) Make the neck, shoulders, and possibly ears a priority. I won't get into nerve endings. When you're in bed with a woman, you can't reference a textbook to find them. But I do know that *every woman has spots above her waist that turn her on.* You just have to find them. The neck, shoulders, and ears are good places to start, as they're most common—kinda like R, S, T, L, N, and E on *Wheel of Fortune*. But occasionally she'll have a spot like her elbow or her eyebrow or something—and you should seek it out. You'll be rewarded greatly when you do (like guessing an "X" on *Wheel of Fortune* and having the answer inexplicably be "Xeroxed Xerxes").

(8) Never pounce down below. I would have no problem with my penis being touched 24 hours a day. Context be damned; business meetings, funerals, anti-penis-touching rally, whatever.

---

[175] Yeah, I just admitted that I got information for this book from *10 Things I Hate About You.* Whatever. I have it on good authority that *Tuesdays with Morrie* was basically plagiarized from *The Breakfast Club.*

It's why men spend so much effort trying to induce penis touching. It works at any occasion, like a deli tray.

Women need context. You can't just pounce when she's not warmed up. It's like trying to cook a quiche without preheating the oven (I assume). So give her plenty of time to get in the right frame of mind before you start in.

(9) If she tries to talk dirty or do something experimental, never, ever laugh. Even the most outgoing women can be self-conscious in bed. Especially when it comes to introducing things into the mix that are ostensibly taboo. *When she dirty talks, she's putting herself out there.* If you laugh at her, not only will she be scared of dirty talking in the future, she also may be scared to initiate *anything* innovative for a long time.

So be kind and receptive, even if her dirty talking sounds like a mix between a high school sex-ed textbook and bad amateur porn ("Ooh baby, do you like when I touch your perineum? Yeah you like that. My labia majora are secreting. Does that make you hot? You are no longer flaccid, so I believe it does.").

(10) Avoid the belly button. For some reason, women just always seem to hate when you interact with their belly buttons. I hypothesize that it's *some mixture of stomach insecurity and bad memories of vicious raspberries* from siblings.

So stay away from it. Who cares about the belly button anyway? At the risk of sounding like a really crude Jedi, that's not the hole you're looking for.

(11) Don't profusely apologize if you finish prematurely. Yes, it's humiliating to finish early. But instead of talking as fast as you can about how that's never happened before and you're so sorry and you'll make it up to her in 20 minutes[176] . . . at least you

---

[176] That number is for a 25-year-old. Add four minutes to this total for every extra year you've been alive beyond that.

can *make a token effort to spin it under the "it just felt too good, you're just too hot" umbrella.*

That, at least, keeps a shred of sexiness alive—and maybe she'll be cool with it and let you help try to polish her off manually. When you start apologizing, you become so quickly unattractive that all of the momentum she's built up will vanish.

11 Sex Tricks and Techniques
Men Will Absolutely Love

There's a reason that every issue of *Cosmopolitan* in history has a cover story focusing on "Tips to Please Your Man."[177] Clearly, their market research has shown you're not buying it because of the cover photo of Ashlee Simpson-Wentz, Holly Robinson-Peete, or Mark Linn-Baker. You're buying it for those tips.

Here are tips that may or may not have ever appeared in *Cosmo*— I'm assuming that, at this point, even *they* can't keep track.

(1) Love your body as much as he does (or at least pretend to). When you're about to get it on with a guy, he doesn't know that you've gained four pounds in the past year. He can't see those couple of stretch marks by your armpits or the ever-so-subtle size difference in your breasts. He just wants to see you naked.

So if you go ahead and boldly strip off those clothes for him, *your laundry list of microscopic and sometimes imaginary flaws will be completely wiped out.* You know what *will* make him notice them? Your pointing them out.

(2) Start foreplay hours before, in public. Male foreplay is different than female foreplay. A guy doesn't necessarily need you to kiss his neck for five minutes in bed—but he *does want to believe it's taking everything in your power not to just rip off his*

---

[177] How boring must the monthly editorial pitch meetings be there: "I was thinking: 43 tips to please your man in bed." "Ooh, I was actually thinking something pretty similar: 29 tips for mind-blowing sex." "Wow, you guys must be inside my brain. I was thinking: 51 secrets to make your man beg for more." Then the editor green lights 'em all, someone calls Eva Longoria-Parker to be on the cover, and the lead story for the month is "123 Amazing Sex Tips."

clothes and have your way with him right there in the middle of Arby's. Deep down, he knows it's not true . . . but he likes to pretend.

So if you do quick, little things in public to let him know that you're dying to have the sex with him, it's the best foreplay he'll ever get. Try giving him a quick flash when no one's looking, reaching into his front pocket so your hand is brushing against his stuff, or sending him a dirty text when you're sitting across the table from each other at a crowded restaurant.

(3) Pay attention to the testicles. As young boys, we learn quickly that our number one priority in life is just to avoid getting

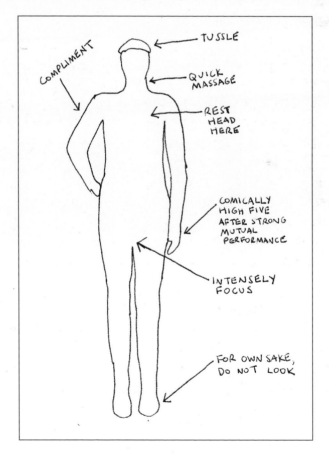

COMPLIMENT

TUSSLE

QUICK MASSAGE

REST HEAD HERE

COMICALLY HIGH FIVE AFTER STRONG MUTUAL PERFORMANCE

INTENSELY FOCUS

FOR OWN SAKE, DO NOT LOOK

hit in the balls. A day cannot be considered a total failure, even if the only productive thing you accomplish is protecting your balls from an attack.

The side effect here is that we get extraordinarily nervous—and therefore extraordinarily excited and turned on—when we finally allow someone to have full, unregulated access to our testicles. *It's the sexual equivalent of bungee jumping.* Odds are nothing's going to go wrong and we're just going to have a rush. But if something gets tucked or yanked or snapped wrong, it's an unparalleled disaster.

So include them when you're fishing around down there. They provide a whole different set of sensations.

(4) Make getting undressed into a show. *Think of your body as a Benihana.* Sure, we want to eat the beef and chicken and fried rice, but part of the experience is seeing the whole show that leads up to eating that beef. (That ended up *way* dirtier than I initially intended it to be.)

(5) Join in on the touching. Guys with a little experience know two things: (1) the female orgasm is *not* a myth, regardless of what our grandfathers told us; and (2) we have almost no ability to get you there without your help. I could quote statistics here on orgasms achieved from clitoral stimulation versus orgasms achieved from just plain old back-and-forth, but that's Globetrotters-Generals.

So, please, use your hand, use a toy, use a long-stemmed rose, but *never hesitate to help out.* If a guy's offended that he and he alone can't rhythmically pound you into bliss, that's a clear window into other future relationship issues.

(6) Early on, fake it if you must. That's right. I'm actually about to advocate faking orgasms. Continuing on from the previous point, we desperately want you to have an orgasm. If you don't, we feel horrible. If you do, we feel like we're the Greek god of sex, reincarnated.[178]

Let's assume the first few times you have sex with a new person, things aren't great—you don't know or understand each other, you're nervous, you're trying to make a good impression, he's going too fast and seems off his game. All of that adds up—and could very well mean you don't climax. But if he's trying his best and you can tell he's got good technique buried in there somewhere, fake it and *give him the confidence* that things are going well. That should loosen him up so he paces himself and performs better next time around.[179]

(7) Make a surprisingly freaky offer. It's the old Madonna/whore thing.[180] The *dream woman is the one who's a proper lady in public but goes absolutely crazy in bed.* As a woman trying to fulfill that role, you don't have to go over the top, like wearing a pantsuit on a date, then stripping it off at home to reveal you've been packing electrified nipple clamps and a *very* confused live chicken underneath, but offer a little something up that lets him know you've got a wild side.

A few ideas: Maybe you could bring your own toy along in your purse on a date, or ask him if you can watch porn together, or tell him where you want him to finish. All of those might literally make his jaw drop.[181]

(8) Give status updates. Assume he's concentrating diligently on trying to finish at the same time or after you. So *giving him*

---

[178] Turns out the Greek god of sex is Dionysus. I always thought it was Uncle Jesse Katsopolis.

[179] This will backfire if he has bad technique. So only do this whole faking thing if it's clear he's got some skills but is nervous and/or doesn't quite understand your preferences yet.

[180] No, younger readers, I didn't just refer to Madonna as a "whore thing." Consult your local library for clarification. And, while there, if there's a secretly naughty librarian, she'll doubly illustrate what I'm talking about.

[181] Ever seen a really turned-on ventriloquist's dummy? His jaw will drop like that (doubly so if you goose him like a ventriloquist's dummy).

status updates on your progress will help his pace consid-
erably. It's the Facebook era. If you give him status updates, he'll
appreciate them so much that he'll click the "Like" button . . . *in*
his mind. (That line sounds less stupid if you say "in his mind" in a
deep, echoing James Earl Jones voice.)

**(9) Try to be the aggressor and initiate at least one-third
of the time.** There's a reason that somewhere around 80 percent
of porn scenes involve a woman initiating sex with a man. It's what
men really, really want (and don't usually get).

And yes, you're thinking, *well, 80 percent of porn scenes also
feature men with completely hairless bodies and women with
horrible tattoos, so should he wax his body while I get a tattoo
covering my entire back featuring a skeleton fighting a panda?* No.
Pick and choose what you copy from porn.

(10) Include oral in foreplay . . . forever. An old husband's
tale says there's an inversely proportional relationship between the
length of a relationship and the amount of blow jobs given. (There's
also an inversely proportional relationship between describing
blow-job frequency with the term "inversely proportional relationship" and receiving blow jobs, but that's neither here nor there.)

Well—and I mean this in the most motivational and least double
entendre-d way possible—suck it up. *Nothing keeps him excited
about having sex with you for decades like the knowledge
that oral sex is part of the package.*

(11) Give him a compliment afterward. After sex, when
reality sets back in, he wants to make sure (1) you had a great
time; (2) you're totally satisfied; (3) you're not freaked out by any
of the stuff he said or did; and (4) *he's achieved or retained
the crown of Best Lover You've Ever Had.* By giving him a
compliment, you assuage all four simultaneously.

It doesn't have to be an original compliment every time. ("You
know how twelve minutes and thirteen seconds in when you ran

your right hand down my left side? That was a creative and memorable move.") A simple "That was amazing" is all he needs.

11 Secrets for Taking
Amazing Nude Photos

I've never posed for nude photos. (There's not a white balance in the world that can account for my skin.) But I have looked at millions of nude photos. I have enough film production experience to know what does and doesn't flatter the body. And one time I took a couple of nude photos of someone I was dating. No, not while she was asleep. No, I didn't save copies. Yes, I did initially broach the subject by saying it was "research."[182]

(1) Don't take the photos yourself. MySpace has done a lot of damage to the world. But beyond setting Web design back a solid 12 years and giving hope to millions of terrible amateur rappers, its *true* sin was making people think it was OK to extend their arm as high into the air as possible to take a self-portrait.

Yes, you look better from a super-high angle. It hides every chin except your primary one and up to 240 pounds. But your nude photos shouldn't include you reaching as high as you can. Beyond the deception you're perpetrating, it's not sexy when your elbow looks like it's about to pop out because you're hyperextending your arm.

Have someone else take your photos. *He/she will be able to capture you from multiple angles and from multiple distances.* If you don't want to bring in anyone else for your naked

---

[182] "Research" is a very clever way to talk someone into nude photos. However . . . it's only a fraction as effective as saying the photos are for "art." If you have even a remote shred of artistic credibility, use it as a springboard into taking nude photos of everyone you can. Then call your parents and let them know that art history degree you have *was* good for something.

photo shoot, at least put your camera on a tripod or a stack of books and use the timer.

(2) Get *very* aggressive on your blemishes. Today's cameras pick up everything: razor bumps, redness from fresh waxing, splotchy teeth, C-section scars, that one black hair growing near your nipple, stretch marks, varicose veins, and wrinkles. And, odds are, you're not good enough with Photoshop or airbrushing to fix them afterward.[183]

By waxing/plucking/spray-removing hair the day before, you can fix some of the blemishes you'd get from day-of hair removal. You can get around the rest of the stuff with liberal use of makeup. (Yes, guys, too.[184])

The most important reason to fix all this stuff is because you *must* be confident for the photos. *If you're embarrassed or (overly) self-conscious and holding back, it'll show.*

(3) Don't eat on shoot day. From what I've gathered in talking with the occasional actor, actress, or Sears catalog model, everyone of both genders avoids eating before a shoot. By not eating, you'll (1) look better without a meal puffing out your belly and (2) more important, *feel* like you look better. It comes back to that confidence thing. And *nothing says "confidence" like that delirious light-headed feeling* that comes from only drinking half a Diet Coke that day.

(4) Think long and hard before you decide to include your face. The biggest decision you have to make is whether you

---

[183] No offense intended. Very few people are good enough with those to fix minor blemishes in photos. It's like if you were going up in space and I suggested you might not be a great astronaut. It's not that you couldn't be a great astronaut, it's just that very few people have astronaut training.

[184] Get this stuff called concealer. It's in the makeup aisle of the store. Whenever I buy it, I take out my cell phone and have a fake conversation with my girlfriend, pretending I'm buying it for her. Very effective technique.

want your face included in these photos. Some people don't have a problem with nude photos of them existing in the world. I, personally, do. The classy dames on *Girls Gone Wild* who sign away the lifetime rights to their nude image in exchange for a $4 tank top clearly do not. Let's break down the pros and cons.

Reasons to include your face:

Your eyes dictate the sexiness of the photos, arguably more than the body.

It's *much less sexy to look at a nude photo where the head's missing.*

If you're considering nude photos, you're clearly confident with your physical appearance, and some of that confidence stems from your facial attractiveness.

By taking out the face the photos go from "erotic" to "OK, that's a decapitated nude body . . . ?"

If it looks like your head's chopped off and you don't have a jack-o-lantern under your arm, the recipient(s) of the photos can't even make the "Ichabod Crane" joke you totally know they would.

Reasons to not include your face:

Exponentially increases your plausible deniability if (and, let's be honest, when) the photos get out into the world.

If you ever wind up on a reality show, your ex won't be able to make six figures selling the copies of the photos (that he "promised he tore up") to *US Weekly*.

You can get kinkier if your face isn't associated.

You can always wear a mask and go for an *Eyes Wide Shut* theme.

However, you might have to explain *Eyes Wide Shut* to the recipient of the photos or, even worse, sit through it with them.

(5) Pick a space and clean it. On my website, I once compiled a list of sexy photos ruined by things in the background. It was crazy. I found pictures online of women who posed in underwear with their sleeping dad, confused toddler, or unflushed toilet in the background.

So, before you shoot, *get everything even remotely unsexy out of the room:* family photos, *Scarface* posters, garbage, unmade bedsheets, your kid. Almost no stuff is ideal. You can use props, but shooting in an extremely clean, minimalist space guarantees the focus will stay on you.[185]

(6) Lighting 101. Rather than write an essay about how to properly light photos, I'm going to just give three quick pointers.[186] I feel like they'll stick better that way, which is good—because if you eff up the lighting, you will hate the way you look in the photos, develop a complex about how you look naked, and start wearing denim cutoffs when you shower.

(1) *Do not use the flash. The flash is not your friend.* It's not even your acquaintance. It's harsh, it screws up your eyes, and it will wash you out and make you look terrible. So turn off the flash and light yourself a different way.

(2) *Use soft light.* Take the lamps you have and put white tissue paper over them to diffuse them. This makes the light soft, forgiving, and sexy.

(3) *The sun is the best light source there is.* Of course, this means taking nude photographs outdoors, which puts you at a risk of someone else . . . well, taking nude photographs of you (and probably with a better camera).

(7) Go for black-and-white. *This will help you plead the "art" defense* if your mom, grandma, boss, pastor, or political opponent somehow gets his/her hands on the photos. You're

---

[185] And that your photo won't circulate the Internet where some blogging jackass can scoop it up and write a few bitchy one-liners about it.

[186] I hope this very, very, very basic Lighting 101 lesson will help you avoid making a gaffe. Get it? GAFFE?

looking for *Playboy* here or, at the worst, Cinemax. Color photos can start venturing into *Hustler* territory.

Black-and-white nude photos are, generally, artistic (unless you're taking super-extreme close-ups of your genitalia).

(8) Be very, very careful with super-extreme close-ups of your genitalia. Because it will, literally,[187] *destroy* you if you take a bunch of nude photos, you hand them to your boyfriend, he's looking through them with a huge smile on his face, then *flips to a photo taken three inches from your vulva and instinctively recoils.*[188]

(9) Pick proper angles and shots. Experiment with lots of different angles during your shoot, because you never know what's going to work. But, in general, there are a few angles that should be avoided at all costs:

(1) *From below*—This camera angle could give Tom Hanks in *Philadelphia* a double chin. Or Tom Hanks in *The Da Vinci Code* a quintuple chin.

(2) *Bent over from behind*—**Human beings were not meant to be viewed bent over, from behind.** At least not in photo form. You'll freak out that your buttocks seem to expand out and cover the entire width of the photo (even if the telephoto lens is used). And, unless you're full-out Brazilianed, be prepared to see hair you never needed to see.

(3) *With you scrunched over*—Extending your body is flattering. Scrunching your body down is not.

(10) Don't look at your photos halfway through. I can't recommend this enough. The single best way to be self-conscious (other than your little brother busting in on your shoot and yelling

---

[187] Figuratively.

[188] Or, worse, says, "Feeeed me, Seymour!"

"You look like a fat asshole!") is to scroll through the camera halfway through the shoot.

As the shoot progresses, you'll *get into that zone of relaxation, experimentation, and confidence.* Seeing your photos will jar you out of it.

As a human being, there's no one more critical of your body than you. (At least until you become a celebrity, and then everyone in the world is more critical of your body than you.)

(11) Make a plan for the future of the photos. Naked photos of you now exist. You need to have a plan. Will you download them onto your computer, print them once, and then delete the files off your hard drive and camera? Did you use a Polaroid? Will you put them on your cell phone to "sext"?[189]

Whatever your plan is, *take whatever privacy measures you can,* to give yourself a chance that they won't fall into the wrong hands. Because there's a 99.996 percent chance they will. But if you don't take these precautions, that jumps up to 99.999 percent.

---

[189] I find the term "sext" to be cringe worthy and regret having used it in this book.

11 Times and Places Where You Can Be Sexually Casual without Judgment

I am orienting this list more toward women than men. Full blame goes to society. While the hooking up/casual sex lifestyle continues to gain momentum every day—promoted, naturally, by the Liberal Media—society still staunchly takes the position that it's OK for single men to try to stick it in as many places as possible, but women still need to keep their number down.

On a day-to-day basis, we, as humans, are not supposed to go around banging strangers.[190] And, in general, our grandmothers and the Jonas Brothers would like to think we only have sex with someone once we're married to him/her.

Of course, that doesn't happen. Most of the people I've met view being single as a ticking clock at the sexual buffet of life—you get to date different people, try different things, and make different mistakes before you settle into glorious monogamy.[191]

So here are 11 times and places where you can go ahead and have a one-night stand, a casual encounter, a random hookup with someone whose name you think might be "Tio"—and do it without enduring too much judgment from the masses.

(1) Las Vegas. It's the only American city with a marketing campaign centered on casual sex;[192] the "What happens in Vegas,

---

[190] Unless we're humans living in the Roman Empire or New York City as it was portrayed on *Friends*. Ever watch the reruns of that show? My GOD did nineties sitcoms portray adult life as some kind of glorious, consequence-free orgy.

[191] Monogamy is like the Italian restaurant next to the buffet. Your days of variety are over, and now it's spaghetti every night for the rest of your life. Emotionally fulfilling spaghetti.

[192] Even more than Intercourse, Pennsylvania.

stays in Vegas" slogan isn't referring to all the great family memories you'll make visiting quilting museums.

And we buy into it. *In Vegas, people have a mentality shift for the weekend.* They go from "responsible adult" to "I could get in a little trouble and, as long as I don't end up with alcohol poisoning, a second mortgage, that tattoo of a skeleton fighting a panda I saw in that porno, any STD more severe than chlamydia, or a dead hooker in the closet, I'm going to let it fly."

People seem more open to one-night stands there than they are back in real life. After all, your friends are out there hooking up, too; you won't want to be the one without a crazy adventure to share the next day at lunch.

(2) On an overseas trip. You're *supposed* to expand your sexual horizons when you travel overseas. It's the privilege that comes with spending two months' rent on a plane ticket. No one will judge you if you travel halfway across the world and have *a torrid, one-week love affair with a mysterious swarthy stranger* who may or may not be a pirate. (A romanticized pirate, swashbuckling, treasure maps, parrot on the shoulder, etc.—not a Somalian with a semiautomatic machine gun.)

(3) With one, and only one, celebrity. Everyone's entitled to one past hookup with name recognition—just one. One celebrity, you've got a cool story. *Two or more, and whispers start about your self-respect issues.* (Partially because people will start mumbling about star-intercoursing . . . and partially because one of the two will probably be Zach Braff and, ya know, come on.)

(4) Directly after a breakup or divorce. Your first post-breakup sexual encounter is a freebie, no matter *what* the person looks like. *As long as it's not with one of your ex's friends* or siblings—your ex's siblings, not yours—you're probably in the clear.

(5) The first time you drink Red Bull and vodka. By about age 22, most people have figured out what alcohol does to their body.

If I drink X amount, my body reacts this way; if I drink Y amount, it reacts differently; if I drink Z amount plus do shots of T or J or E, it reacts even worse.

None of that prepares you for the mix of energy drinks and alcohol.[193] It hits you in an entirely different way than just drinking beers or cocktails—or even shots. So, the first time, if you go a bit crazier than normal and make more controversial decisions than normal, people will reluctantly, but definitively, give you a free pass.

God, however, will not give you a pass, so as you lay in bed, drunk but unable to go to sleep, heart pounding dangerously hard, you'll have to talk things out with Him.[194]

(6) After a once-in-a-lifetime date. You know it when you're on the date. Where the guy clearly put in an incredible amount of planning, effort, and money, and everything's just magical like the unicorns at the petting zoo on Fairytale Island.

That's the date where you'll have a realization: "I don't know if I see myself ending up with this guy—he's totally wrong for me and I think he called the waiter 'chief'—but *when I look back at this incredible night, I want the memories to be topped off by an equally amazing sexual experience.*"

You're completely right—it should. And all of your friends will agree when you relate the story to them the next day; none of them would've handled it differently.

(7) After the death of an immediate family member. Not that you'll be thinking, "Well, I sure am gonna miss Dad, but at least I can go bang someone for comfort and a distraction without anyone

---

[193] Drinking your first Red Bull and vodka is just like the when you saw *Avatar* in 3-D. Your horizons are permanently expanded, and you're left with a raging headache.

[194] Or Her. I've been doing gender-neutral for this whole book, might as well not stop when it comes to talkin' God.

judging me," but, at least, keep that in the back of your mind. *Silver linings,* friends. Silver linings.

(8) When you're trying to prove that the person you've been dating for a while isn't your boy/girlfriend. You get a pass here for two reasons: (1) you're asserting your singleness—which they'll like, because it means you're still a soldier in the Single Army, guaranteed to stay fun and not become one of those people who ends up in a relationship, then goes AWOL forever.

And (2) *you're not just having sex for sex's sake; you're proving a point.* When you do something with conviction and principles (even if "I'm proving I'm not in a committed relationship" is about the loosest definition of "principle" ever), you claw your way to some high ground.

(9) The time you go on a date with someone who's really hot but *really* dumb. At some point, I hope you get the chance to go out with someone who's amazingly attractive—even if he/she has zero other redeeming qualities.[195] Terrible personality, dumb as an ox (and not just any ox, but an ox whose parents are cousins), and shows signs of certifiable insanity, likes Chris Rock more as a movie star than stand-up.

You should absolutely do what it takes to get physical with the person once, and, from that point on, *only go for encores if they don't have to include things like meals,* conversation, or spending the night.

Everyone deserves to see what it's like to hook up with someone who's got the body of a mannequin . . . even if he/she's got the personality of one, too.[196]

---

[195] Sure, it would be nicer to wish that you could go out with someone who's amazingly attractive and also has a great personality, but, I'm sorry to say, Ron Howard's already got a wife.

[196] But not a mannequin that's actually an Egyptian princess reincarnated.

(10) On an international flight. A friend of mine (name redacted) joined the mile-high club with a stranger on an international flight. I thought her rationale was infallible.

On her flight, she was seated next to a guy whom she describes as "superhot."[197] They started talking. And talking. They talked for the next 10 hours straight. That's when things started escalating, and they started discussing making a trip to the most romantic place on Earth—an airplane bathroom.[198] Her thought process went like this: "We've talked for 10 hours. *If you think about it, that's the equivalent of four or five dates.* If I'd gone on four or five dates with this guy, we'd probably be having sex. So I'm going to jump on this once-in-a-lifetime opportunity."

And she was absolutely right. They made the world's most uncomfortable love in the airplane bathroom, parted ways after the flight, and never saw each other again. And she never regretted a thing.

(11) When you're still a virgin junior year of college or later. Because no one can say, "It's about damn time, *I was starting to think you were asexual or a monk*" and judge you in the same breath.

---

[197] When I responded, "OMG, how hawt was he? Did he look like one of the Hanson brothers?" she rolled her eyes and said, "Do you want the story for your book or not? You do? Good. Then shut the fuck up."

[198] And not just any airplane bathroom but one that had just experienced 10 consecutive hours of international travelers punishing it.

11 Tips for Proposing, Wrangling, and Shining during a Threesome

At some point, everyone's wondered, "Would I want to have a threesome?" And that's mightily impressive for something that's pretty far up there on the sexual adventurousness scale. I mean, not everyone has thought, "Would I want to dress up in a child's Robin costume, jam a lemon wedge in my mouth, and tie a rope around my neck while I pleasure myself to the music of Savage Garden?" And that's only like four or five notches more advanced than a threesome.

So, for those that have pondered that question—the threesome one, not the autoerotic asphyxiation/"Truly Madly Deeply" one—here's how to bring one up, make one happen, and not screw things up when you do.

(1) Women are 95 percent responsible for a threesome happening; men are 95 percent responsible for screwing one up. Yes, a guy can plant the "you want to have a threesome" seed in a woman's mind, *Inception*-style.[199] But when you get down to it, a woman has to make three major decisions for a threesome to happen:

(1) *Am I OK with sharing my boyfriend/husband/man-du-jour with another woman?* (2) I know the ups and downs of the vagina, am I really ready to cross that frontier? (3) Am I so devoted to making this happen that I'm willing to go out there and find another woman for us?

---

[199] At least I think that's what *Inception* was about. If you told me the whole movie was actually just an allegory for the Bolshevik Revolution I'd probably believe that, too.

If she enthusiastically answers "yes" to all three questions, it's going to happen. And between that moment and the moment when all three of you are naked, the only thing that can really go wrong is the guy saying something dumb/inappropriate/offensive/insensitive/creepy. Basically, anything, really. Your best bet might be a vow of silence from agreement to commencement.

(2) A woman has to do the recruiting. As I hinted in the previous point, it takes a woman to sell another woman on a threesome. It's because, essentially, *the guy is just a prop.* Both women involved have been with guys; guys aren't new and exciting. They're both going to be more concerned with the other woman— that's the less familiar and more taboo ground.[200]

(3) Establish clear ground rules beforehand. It's a perfectly acceptable ground rule for a woman to say, "You can do anything with the other girl except for actual sex." Or if your girlfriend is Julia Roberts, she'd say, "You can do anything with her except for kissing."

Regardless of what your final rules look like, make sure to have the discussion beforehand. If you're in a committed relationship and are, therefore, *essentially cheating on your significant other right in front of him/her,* there can be disastrous consequences if you do something he/she wasn't mentally prepared for.

(4) By the grace of God, the hotter a woman is, the more likely she is to be into it. My most threesome-savvy friend (who asked for off-the-record anonymity) proposed this theory, and I think it's wonderful. *Incredibly attractive women are bored*

---

[200] It's like when you're about to start a new job. You know once you're at your desk you'll be fine because you know how to do the job. It's the other stuff—where do you park, what do you wear, how much terrible and allergy-inducing perfume will the women in adjacent cubicles wear—that makes you worried. In a threesome, the actual job is the guy, and the parking lot, clothing choice, and perfume wearers are the women. There's a reason this metaphor is in a footnote and didn't make it into the actual body copy.

with men. They've had men. Men are less beautiful than them, even beautiful men. So, because the media has reiterated over and over and over that casual lesbianism isn't just OK, but it's an encouraged rite of passage, they start thinking about other beautiful women as a potential option. Keep this in mind when you're recruiting, and don't be afraid to aim high.

On a side note, this also seems like a good spot to discuss an underrated benefit of threesomes: They take any inkling of a desire to cheat and destroy it.

Not to say that we're all just ticking bombs waiting to cheat with the first tattoo artist, tennis instructor, or au pair we see. But committed monogamy makes *any* sexual variety deeply forbidden, and, thanks to human nature, that makes it *way* more tempting. So just *knowing* that a threesome possibility exists strips the forbiddenness away . . . and makes it far less intoxicating. Basically, it's using one taboo (a threesome) to completely eliminate a much more emotionally damaging taboo (adultery). Let's see autoerotic asphyxiation do *that.*

(5) Pay equal attention to both other people. You never want to get to a scenario where two of the participants are going at it hard and *the other person has to wonder if he/she should run out to the store and grab everyone some Gatorade.* (This is monumentally amplified when the person getting ignored is your significant other.)

(6) A no-touch threesome is better than no threesome at all. There's a hierarchy of threesomes. On the top is two women and one guy and at the very bottom is one woman and two guys who've made a prior handshake agreement not to make any form of contact—eye contact, physical contact, or verbal contact.[201]

---

[201] I believe in some circles the two guys-one girl threesome is referred to as the Devil's Threeway. And while it does sound horrible, the two guys—one girl threesome *is* better than the two girls—one cup threesome.

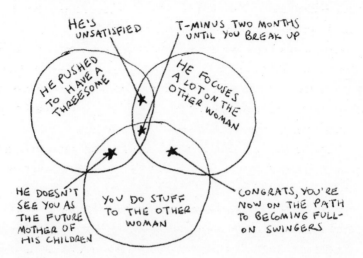

Somewhere in the middle is the ultimate "my boyfriend wants a threesome but I am reluctant" compromise: two women who have free reign to go nuts on each other, and the guy can only touch and be touched by his girlfriend. As a guy, *if you get that offer, jump on it.* If you hesitate, you'll start a massive fight ("Why is that not good enough? Is this really about you getting to be with another woman?").

(7) Have answers prepared for the big "Why do you want a threesome?" questions. Here are the questions that come up when a guy proposes a threesome:

"Am I not enough for you?" Answer: "Of course. *You're perfect, and our sex life is amazing.* This has always been a fantasy of mine and, I kinda suspect, a fantasy of yours. I just don't know if there's anyone out there who could handle us!"

"Could you really take me seriously as the mother of your children after watching me go down on another woman?" Answer: "Well, I'd definitely never forget that image—but it would just make

me more into you. *Zero* judgments. We'll just keep it loose, and casual, and fun. I definitely won't overthink it."

"Are you saying you want us to become swingers?" Answer: "Absolutely not. I don't want to swap you to some creepy dude so I can be with his ugly wife. I just want us to fulfill this fantasy, one time, so we can have the experience and then go right back to just you and me, like things should be."

"What if I wanted to do one with another man and you?" Answer: "Only if I get to do stuff with the guy." (That will stop her *dead* in her tracks.)

(8) Don't expect the gracefulness you see in porn. In porn, everyone in a threesome is a veteran. They have a director telling them what to do. They might even practice beforehand. You have none of that. Limbs are going to flail all over the place, people are going to try getting into positions but then break them because they're too uncomfortable, and at points it's going to be way more physically challenging than sexually stimulating.

In fact, *do a lot of stretches beforehand.* You're probably going to end up doing more squats, push-ups, leg lifts, and hand-stands than you've done since you were in grade school and quit gymnastics lessons after three ill-fated weeks.

(9) If you decide to pay for the third participant, spend the money to make it worthwhile. If you're lucky, you've got whatever the threesome equivalent of gaydar is—threedar?—and that guides your recruiting process. But if you do decide that you want to bring in a professional as your third participant, get ready to spend (some very worthwhile) money. You want to *go for the kind of escort who mysteriously gets appointed to a position like Special Adviser to the Lieutenant Governor*—not the kind whom you pick up outside a Costco and only agrees to partici-pate if she doesn't have to take off her Kenny Chesney T-shirt.

(10) Don't push too hard for girl-on-girl stuff if it's not happening. So you're in the middle of a threesome. Both women are touching you, and you're having a gay old time. But they're not. Don't be too pushy about them kissing or doing things with each other—*there's a very good reason why they're not.* One or both is *not* into it, and they know it. Your pushing is just going to make everyone uncomfortable for the entire time . . . and, if things get too awkward, the greatest moment in your life (arguably) might get cut short.[202]

(11) Afterward, don't mention threesomes again for at least six months. Your best chance of having another threesome is to *completely undersell the impact this threesome had on your life.* After the third participant leaves, don't break down into tears and start giving the equivalent of an Oscar acceptance speech. ("I just want to thank Jesus, my parents for doing such a selfless job raising me, and my girlfriend Erin. We did it, baby!")

The correct thing to say is something to the effect of, "That was a lot of fun. Now let's get back to doing what we do best and focusing on each other." Don't bring it up again until at least six months later. Then, as soon as *anything* happens regarding the threesome—he/she mentions your third participant, you try a move you haven't used since then, you're watching the movie *Threesome* with Stephen Baldwin[203]—broach the topic of maybe doing another one sometime in the future.

---

[202] Unless you scored four touchdowns in one game at Polk High, or you won a crazy eating challenge (like finish the 12-foot sub in 30 minutes or less and it's free), this is your peak.

[203] Not watching with him. He was in it. Unless you're having sex with Stephen Baldwin and watching his own movie with him.

11 Best and Worst Places
to Have Sex in Public

This hopelessly idealistic guy I knew back in college had a quote in his e-mail signature from Calvin and Hobbes: "It's a magical world, Hobbes ol' buddy. Let's go exploring." He took this quote to be symbolic of the curiosity of the human spirit. I have decided to co-opt it to be the introduction to my list about banging it out in parking lots and coatrooms. I guess that quote's ambiguous enough that it can mean whatever you need it to mean.[204]

(1) GOOD: A park you can walk to (that isn't a mecca for experimental married men). Let's dissect this piece-by-piece:

"A park"—At night, under the stars,[205] soft grass, romantic.

"You can walk to"—Parking a car can draw the attention of the police. In general, *when having sexual relations in public, you want to avoid the cops* at all costs.

"That isn't a mecca for experimental married men"—According to the Internet, there are all sorts of men making anonymous love in public parks, many of whom have wives back at home (and constituents back in their district). Parks are the truck stops of the Craigslist era. No judgments here. But if the cops *do* run a sting operation that sweeps up three dozen gay men . . . and one hetero couple . . . that's one of those news stories that gets passed around online like crazy.[206]

---

[204] And I assume there's a demographic out there who thought, "Calvin and Hobbes? You mean the guy pissin' on the Chevy logo?"

[205] Or under the romantic haze of light pollution, depending on where you live.

[206] It'd be as bad as you guys spotting a leprechaun in Alabama. Or having some little British kid

(2) GOOD: A movie theater with about a dozen other people. If the theater's empty and an employee wanders in, he'll see you. If it's too crowded that isn't good, either—someone will be sitting close enough to pick you up with at least one of his/her senses (let's hope it isn't taste). The best bet is to *sit in the back of a movie theater that has a few other people scattered around* throughout.[207]

And make sure to pick an appropriate, R-rated movie—there's something about having sex in the back row of *The Adventures of Sharkboy and Lavagirl* that feels so unwholesome.

(3) BAD: The beach. Don't be misled by the deliciousness of the drink called Sex on the Beach. For that drink to be *accurately* named, while you sipped it, someone would come up and *jam sand into every orifice on your body.* Beyond that aspect, police tend to patrol beaches at night much more aggressively than places like parks, since beaches have less harmless man-on-man action and more people drowning.[208]

(4) GOOD (BUT GROSS): The men's bathroom. At a bar or restaurant or stadium, it's to be rank. *Rank.* But you should opt for the men's room, because women will freak out if a guy steps out of a stall in their bathroom. Whereas a group of drunk guys . . . well, they'll give a standing ovation to a woman who steps out of one of theirs post-coitus. If you can *get past the smell, the complete void of classiness, and the constant background serenade of urine* and people saying "bro," this is totally doable.

---

named Charlie bite you. Or putting on a tight Orange Crush shirt and doing the running man and Soulja Boy dances.

[207] Also, it will make your lives much, much easier if the woman is wearing a skirt. Ever tried taking off your pants in a movie theater? It's as inappropriate as taking your pants off at a Pee Wee football game. (You see what I did there?)

[208] And/or immigrating.

(5) BAD: Anywhere near a school. I don't fully understand what does and doesn't qualify you as a sex offender, but I do know people get *real* sensitive about schools. So even though you're both adults, be wary. Something about *"arrested for having sex outside an elementary school"* means you're going to have a *lot* of 'splaining to do.

(6) GOOD: The back of a limo or taxi. As long as you don't leave stains or kick out a window in the throes of passion, *the driver isn't going to stop you.* In fact, he probably likes it. There's an unspoken agreement: you don't complain about the expensive and inefficient route he's taking, and he keeps an eye on the road.

(7) BAD: Abandoned house. Before I started writing this book, someone sent me a link to a piece on Fox News about good places to have sex in public.[209] And one of their suggestions was an abandoned house.

No! No, no, no, please no. First of all, it's scary as hell. Why not just go have sex at an abandoned hall of mirrors, or next to a lake on the 10th anniversary of the night when a group of sexy teens were mysteriously murdered there? Second of all, *neighbors are surprisingly vigilant* about watching for activity in abandoned houses on their street, because no one wants a group of squatters to move in and turn their block into an opium den. In other words, if the ghouls don't get you, the neighborhood watch will.

(8) GOOD: Near a famous monument. If you're going to have sex in public just one time, might as well have *a great story for your grandkids* (once you get senile enough to start telling sex stories to your grandkids.) While there are some guards, these places are often surprisingly accessible and unattended at night.

---

[209] That channel sure does need to get its mission statement straight.

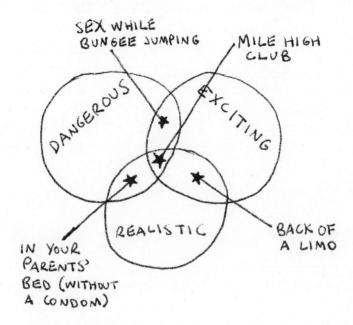

(9) IN BETWEEN: Coatroom. Coatrooms are usually a pretty safe bet at parties and especially at weddings, with two caveats: (1) Either there's no coatroom attendant, you bribe the attendant to leave, or, best of all, you invite him/her to join in; and (2) you have to *do this early enough in the night* that people aren't ready to get their coats and leave yet.

(10) GOOD: Amusement park rides. Ever seen the movie *Fear*, where Mark Wahlberg—back when he was still trying to transition out of his Funky Bunch days—finger-blasted Reese Witherspoon on a roller coaster? According to my girlfriend, that scene was the first time in her life she ever "got tingles down below." And while *roller coasters are good, tunnels of love, lazy rivers, log flumes, and Ferris wheels are even better spots* to do a bunch of funky stuff. Take advantage of those good vibrations. (Come on, come on, come on.)

(11) BAD: Alley. Makes you way too vulnerable. If movies have taught us anything, it's that *as soon as you go into an alley, someone mugs you.* Remember *Batman* (the Michael Keaton one)? Bruce Wayne and his parents got mugged in an alley. His parents got killed, and he ended up becoming a deep-voiced vigilante who spent his whole life searching for a guy who talked about dancing with the devil in the pale moonlight. Do you *really* have time to be a vigilante? Even with a DVR it'd still be really hard to squeeze it in.

11 Rules to Keep a Booty Call
from Getting Messy

If there's one thing that real adults have trouble understanding about everyone Nintendo generation and younger, it's the willingness of our women to enter into no-strings-attached, emotion-free, purely sexual relationships. "Why back in my day," I picture a grown-up *woman* saying, "I wouldn't even neck with a gentleman caller unless he brought my father a two-sheep dowry."[210]

Whatever your reasons are—and there have been many studies on the psychology of booty calls, I'm sure they're in all the medical journals you subscribe to—this list is to help guide you through a booty call where both people are happy, satisfied, and getting exactly what they want.[211]

(1) Do *not* actually make a booty call on the phone. Booty call is an antiquated phrase, like "let's videotape that" or "you don't look like your dad, do you look like the milkman?" Please text. Not only does it save time, on a phone call, *basic courtesy forces you to dance around things* too much. Let's compare:

---

[210] Yeah, everyone 38 years old and up talks like that. You haven't noticed?
[211] Unless you really *do* want that dowry; my "11 Ways to Negotiate the Best Dowry" list got left on the cutting-room floor.

TEXT	PHONE CALL
"You around?"	"Hi!"
"I am . . ."	"Hey."
"Want to get together?"	"What's going on?"
	"Not much."
	"Are you out?"
	"No, got home like a half hour ago."
	"Did you go someplace fun?"
	"Yeah, it was my friend's birthday at this place called Moe's."
	"Oh I think I know that place. Is it on Second?"
	"Yeah!"
	"Right. I was there, man, must've been a few months ago."
	"Oh cool."
	"So what are you up to now?"
	"Not much, I'm just watching a movie."
	"Oh what movie?"
	"*Maid in Manhattan.*"
	"Really?"
	"Yeah."
	"Is it good?"
	"Ha! No, not at all."
	"Ha!"
	"Um"

I'm going to cut the phone call off there because of various word-count restrictions on this book, but suffice to say it goes on for another several banal minutes before small talk ends and you get down to business.

(2) Take turns doing it at each other's places . . . but favor the woman's place. And the reason is simple: Society has told us *it's easier for a guy to say, "I gotta go, I've got a, um . . . thing tomorrow"* and do the Walk Of Shame out of there at four in the morning.[212]

(3) No going to brunch the next day. *When you start eating meals with someone, he/she is no longer a booty call.* You are dating. Even if you split the bill. Even if the meal is Burger King. Even if you sit there in silence. The relationship may be based on sex, but it's still a real relationship.[213]

(4) Make an effort not to spend the night. By the time things wrap up—2, 3, maybe 4 AM—you might just pass out. But if you can muster the strength, *you're doing all parties a favor by getting out of there.* After all, your "um . . . thing" tomorrow is quite important.

Quick note, too: If you do decide to cite the "um . . . thing," and he/she foolishly decides to call you out on it, do have some kind of plan. One time I got called on an "um . . . thing" and blurted out "friend's funeral." That turned an "um . . . thing" into an "um . . . giant ball of lies that took 20 minutes to explain and made me look like a horrible person for having a girl come over for casual sex mere hours before burying a friend." The weirdest part is I've never even *been* to a friend's funeral. I've been lucky. Why that came out of my mouth I don't know. Although I'm sure a psychoanalyst could have an absolute field day with it.

---

212 Citing an "um . . . thing" reminds me of the *South Park* episode where the townspeople commit horrible crimes and then blame them on "some Puerto Rican guy." "Um . . . thing" is the "some Puerto Rican guy" of casual sex.

213 And it's very easy to botch a relationship that's based on sex. Remember when Sandra Bullock proposed that to Keanu Reeves at the end of *Speed*? Clearly she didn't mean it, things got too emotional and, like all relationships born from crises, it flopped—pushing her right into Jason Patric's meaty arms by *Speed 2: Cruise Control*.

(5) You don't have to set things up at 1 AM. Usually, people start trying to make a booty call happen after they've been out for the night and struck out. There's nothing wrong with arranging things earlier in the night. It *might even help you relax when you're out* because it takes some of the pressure off—you're fornicatin' at the end of this night no matter what happens now.[214]

Plus, if you set up a booty call early but something else does develop, it's OK to cancel it. Part of having a no-strings-attached relationship of convenience means last-second cancellations are totally in bounds.

(6) Even if you didn't start as a booty call, you can end as one. Just because you went on a few dates with a person, transitioning into a pure booty call situation isn't completely infeasible. *There are plenty of different types of chemistry.* One very common type? You have terrible conversations but are just fantastic together when you're shacking up.

That situation is just begging for a booty call. Neither of you wants to sit through another two-hour dinner with more uncomfortable pauses than Larry David confronting an imam who took his parking spot. You want to get straight to the denouement.

(7) It's OK to text someone out of the blue. Part of the deal here is that you can have no contact for a few weeks, then make contact randomly and it's fine. *Your success rate might go down*—after a little while with no contact, people tend to reevaluate things—but it's still legal.

If it's been more than a few weeks, here's a trick I use to reestablish contact. It's completely ridiculous and should *not* work . . . yet it's never failed. Send a text around 12:30 AM that says, "Hey did I

---

[214] Plus, how many times in your life do you meet someone, go home with him/her, and have sex? I bet for the average person it's like once or twice, not counting outliers like rock stars or women who have extended periods of That Phase.

just see you at [some location]? I yelled for you but you didn't turn around." Within minutes expect a text back saying, "What? No, I wasn't there!" Contact is reestablished; you're generally face-to-face within 90 minutes.[215]

(8) No breakup call. When it's time for the booty call relationship to end—for whatever reason—you don't have to make a breakup call. *It's a total free pass.*

The next time the other person proposes a get-together you can just text back that you think "we should take a break on this for a little while." And this is a *huge* perk since breakup calls chart just slightly higher than "calling your exes to tell them you have crabs" on the list of Awful Moments in Dating.

(9) Don't leave anything behind. Double-check to make sure you've collected all of your clothes and everything else before you bolt out into the night. That's your policy: *no items left behind.* It's like a much sexier, less divisive cousin of the government's No Child Left Behind thing. (I apologize for mentioning the word "child" in a list about casual sex. And on that note . . .)

(10) Really, use condoms. If there's one time you should absolutely, unequivocally, undisputedly use condoms, it's *when you're having sex with someone you can't even imagine sitting with for a single dinner.*

(11) It's hard, but not impossible, to go from booty call to real relationship. This is *the* big question, and I fall on the side of optimism here. Turning casual sex into . . . um . . . black tie love (?) is quite difficult. But if you do start feeling something for the person (beyond his/her body on top of yours twice a month) and think you guys could have a shot, then go for it.

---

[215] Keep in mind, you can really only pull this trick off once per person. It's like a magician's trick. The first time, everyone's fooled. But if you show someone the trick twice, he/she's going to see where you're hiding the dove in your jacket or the pennies in your coat sleeve.

Test the waters. Next time you're together, find a way to float out the name of a restaurant, or a bar, or a concert or event that's coming up. If he/she ignores your comment, or blows it off—or kinda recoils, even subtly—there's no reciprocation. But *if he/she doesn't seem taken aback,* or even discusses the possibility of maybe going there together, it means that you're not alone in considering the leap.

11 Most Popular Birth Control
Methods, in Order of Effectiveness

Like everyone else, every so often I find myself on various government websites digging through data.[216] Once upon a time, I found myself on the FDA website and found their chart of contraceptives, complete with success ratings. I went through and picked out 11 forms of birth control you might be considering—then ranked them in order of effectiveness.

I won't include abstinence (which is 100 percent effective), because the title refers to popular birth control methods, and ain't nobody calling abstinence popular . . . except maybe the textbooks that the government spent tens of millions of your tax dollars on. Because you know the best way of keeping horny teenagers from getting pregnant? Pretending condoms don't exist.

(1) Implants (99.91% effective when used perfectly/99.91% effective when used imperfectly). And by this I mean an implant that pumps you full of birth control, *not breast implants,* which may have the opposite effect.

Please take note here: Although it seems drastic to get your birth control implanted in you, this is actually ever so slightly better at unwanted pregnancy prevention than getting yourself *sterilized.* And given the choice between the two of them, I'd pick an implant.[217]

---

216 Wait, I'm the only one who does this? I refuse to believe it. Next you're going to tell me I'm the only one who tries to calculate probabilities in his head while he plays Yahtzee on his cell phone. Did you know if your opening roll contains a 2, 3, 4, and 5 you have a 5/9 chance of ending up with a large straight?

217 Given the choice between the three of them I'd choose a seasick crocodile.

(2) Vasectomy/hysterectomy (99.85–99.9% effective when used perfectly/99.5–99.9% effective when used imperfectly). The reason there are two different classes of percentages is because the government breaks down the stats in two ways: If you employ the method perfectly each and every time . . . and if you do it right mostly (but sometimes screw up, like forgetting to take a pill or putting the condom on inside-out or pulling out just half a second too late).

I bring this up here for two reasons: (1) to clarify going forward on this list; and (2) because I'm really not clear how someone could improperly use sterilization. *Unless you do it at home, I'd think it tends to work right.* And if your doctor messes it up, shouldn't it make more than a fraction of a percentage difference?

(3) IUD (99.2–99.9% effective when used perfectly/99.2% effective when used imperfectly). An older version of this list appeared on my website a few years ago and I left off IUDs. I said that I wasn't going to include birth control methods that "no one under 103 years old would use." And that's when I learned that (1) *a lot of women under 103 still use IUDs* and (2) they are surprisingly passionate about their IUDs.

I don't know why I thought they were so old-fashioned. I guess the term "IUD" just makes me picture a late-1800s traveling tonic salesman offering to put one in a woman as a ruse to get her naked in his covered wagon. Anyway, turns out I'm way wrong, and women still swear by these today. So go get your uterus capped like all the other popular girls are doing!

(4) The pill (99.9% effective when used perfectly/95% effective when used imperfectly). I recently learned that *when a girl's cell phone alarm randomly goes off* at, like, 5:30 PM, it's her reminder to herself to take her birth control. Add that to the "secrets women really wish men hadn't figured out" list, right behind Spanx and "I need to wash my hair."

(5) Condoms (97% effective when used perfectly/86% effective when used imperfectly). My high school health teacher told us a story about condoms. A group of health workers went to a village in Africa to teach the people how to use condoms. They demonstrated on a banana. A few months later the pregnancy rate in the village was way up . . . because the guys were just putting condoms on bananas, then putting the bananas on a table and having unprotected sex.

I don't know if the story's true or not.[218] Regardless, I'd guess that *"putting your condom on a bedside banana" qualifies as one of the imperfect methods* of condom usage.

(6) Pullin' out (96% effective when used perfectly/81% effective when used imperfectly). I'm *shocked it's this high*. For all the hype about how pregnancy can happen accidentally even before ejaculation, as long as a guy's got the discipline of a samurai when it's time to withdraw, it's only 1 percent less effective than condoms.[219]

(7) Diaphragms (94% effective when used perfectly/80% effective when used imperfectly). Diaphragms are pretty much done for, at least with the current generation. (At this point, fewer than 2 percent of women using birth control pop in a diaphragm.)

Will they make a retro comeback, like calculator watches, *Tron,* or Mickey Rourke? I doubt it. Will kids in middle school choirs

---

[218] And I'm guessing it's not because, as I was writing this, a friend who went to high school in a totally different part of the country was looking over my shoulder and said, "My health teacher told us that story too, but it was with a pole."

[219] I think this would be a great place to reiterate that the information from this book is for entertainment purposes only and neither the author nor the publisher can be held liable for the results of following this advice. I got these numbers from a government website. I assume they got the numbers from the place the government normally gets its data—running a multimillion-dollar study and then making stuff up to fill in the gaps.

continue to giggle when the teachers tells them to "sing from their diaphragm" from now until the end of time? Indisputably.

(8) The Rhythm Method (91–99% effective when used perfectly/75% effective when used imperfectly). The rhythm method has to do with planning sex around the woman's menstrual cycle. Not, as an anonymous friend of mine once thought, *having sex to house music.*

(9) Female condoms (95% effective when used perfectly/79% effective when used imperfectly). Female condoms look like some kind of unholy jellyfish. And, apparently, *not the kind of jellyfish that are particularly reliable when it comes to preventing pregnancy.*

(10) The sponge (80–91% effective when used perfectly/60–80% effective when used imperfectly). The (ahem) wide deviation in those percentages comes from *whether the woman has birthed a child before or not.* If she hasn't, the sponge is far more effective. But if a baby has traveled down the canal, it never really springs back.

Especially, I'm guessing, if the child has a large head like myself, the late Patrick Swayze, or one of the characters in NBA Jam if you enter the correct code.

(11) Nothin' (15% effective when used perfectly/15% effective when used imperfectly). If you just go ahead and let it fly, you've got a one in seven shot of escaping pregnancy free. *One in seven!* Those are better than the odds of winning a hand of blackjack if the dealer's showing a 7.

Dilemmas

The girl stopped at a red light and looked at me. "I never take guys home," she told me, "but I got into the biggest fight today with my boyfriend because he bought a gun." And, moments later, when she drunkenly grazed her car against a curb somewhere a good 30 miles outside Las Vegas, I said to myself, "I might die tonight."

There have only been three times in my life I've thought I might die. Two months after I got my license when I lost control of my mom's '88 Plymouth Horizon hatchback and found myself skidding down a tree-filled hill; the day in 1996 when I accidentally wandered into an Arab market during a trip to Israel; and that moment in Vegas.

I'd recently broken up with my girlfriend of almost two years. Less than a month later, I found myself on a trip to Vegas with five of my best friends. As it seemingly goes for everyone in a relationship, during the course of those two years, I'd forgotten that women have the capacity to be (sometimes, occasionally) attracted to me. So when, in Vegas, I found myself flirting with—and having success with—women, every switch in my brain flipped off except the raw, primal "me sex now" one.

It's inevitable after a breakup. Breakups do strange things to a person's head. I wasn't hung up on my ex, far from it; with the power of retrospect I was able to see that the relationship lasted longer than it organically should have. When we did break up and she told me her ex-boyfriend from college had been making strong moves toward her for the past few months, I didn't even feel a tinge of jealousy or anger. No, in this case my post-breakup mental shake-up came when I realized that, for the first time in years, I could pursue any woman I wanted to. And, more important, I realized that a few of them wanted me to do just that.

Right after my breakup, I did pretty much everything in this chapter's "11 Things You'll Do in the Month after You Break Up" list. I almost jumped right back into a relationship. I had an awful night hitting on women at a bar that made me question whether I'd ever have sex again. I lost weight. I gained weight. I lost weight. I relapsed and had one encore night with my ex. I hooked up with a questionable girl[220] because I needed to prove to myself I could.

But none of that prepared me for that night in Vegas. My friends and I were out at a bar, and I ended up talking to a local. Ignored the red flag that she was a local hanging out on the Strip (locals rarely seem to do that). Ignored the red flag that she wasn't drinking in a "fun" way—she was drinking with a purpose. Ignored the red flag that, more than once, she mentioned getting rid of her "asshole boyfriend." And ignored the red flag that her friends quickly left the bar, having none of the usual girl qualms about leaving her alone with a strange dude. She was not a normal woman. But, at this point, I was not a normal guy.

We drank, danced, even made out a little bit on the dance floor, as is the style of the time. At the point when she asked me if I wanted to go back to her place, I was officially a single man . . . and a single

---

[220] It's not questionable that she was a girl. She was a questionable choice.

man who was going to have some random, casual sexual relations with a woman he'd just met in Vegas. My friend Nathan, who had watched what was going on, even leaned over and whispered to me at one point, "Welcome back."[221]

Unfortunately, this is when my brain—already in "me sex now" mode—turned that dial up to 11. Any shred of intelligent decision-making was officially gone.

This included: agreeing to go back to her house, somewhere in the outskirts of Vegas, instead of suggesting we go back to my hotel room; not realizing she'd been drinking to the point where her driving was beyond dangerous; and not telling any of my friends I was leaving.

I jolted back to reality—and sobriety—in the car ride, when she went into detail about the boyfriend.

Yes, they'd fought. Yes, it was because he'd bought a gun that day. Yes, he had stormed out, upset about the fight. And just like that, my brain took back control from the unholy penis-alcohol cabal.

It was 5 AM, I was in a car with a girl whose last name I didn't know, she was driving drunk, we were at least a half hour from the Las Vegas strip, and, above all else, there was a decent chance her boyfriend was sitting at her place, waiting to talk or fight things out with her . . . and probably had his brand-new gun with him.

"I might die tonight. I might get shot. What if she pulls up and he's sitting in her parking spot and there I am, some random guy, with his girlfriend? Or what if this is a kidnapping—she seduces a harmless-looking tourist, brings him back, and they hold me for ransom? What will I do?"

I eventually devised a plan. If her boyfriend was there, I was going to jump out of the car and just start running. Never look back.

---

[221] The same Nathan from the intro of this book who compared my penis to Dr. Phil's. He's had some interesting contributions to this book, both on and off the record.

If I get shot in the back like the guy in *Boyz n the Hood* it was my own fault.

I tried to look for landmarks along the drive. I noted major intersections and asked questions about how close we were to her place to try to plan my escape route. I had my cell phone. If he was at her place, I'd run and run and run, calling 911 on the way, trying to make it to a major street. We passed one of those man-made Vegas ponds right by her place. Maybe I could dive in there after calling 911 because water stops bullets? At least I think water stops bullets. At that moment in my life I wish I knew more about water and bullets.

We made it to her apartment complex alive—she only hit the one curb—and, by some mix of luck and divine intervention, the boyfriend wasn't there.[222] We went inside, but, by this point, my loins were completely extinguished. I just wanted to get the hell out of there. This was only exacerbated when we entered her apartment and went to her bed, which was just a mattress on the ground that appeared to be stuffed with hay.[223]

I made up an excuse that my flight was leaving at 9:00 AM, so I had to leave for the hotel in two hours. We laid down on her hay-filled mattress and I pretended to pass out.

She fell asleep shortly thereafter . . . I waited a few minutes . . . said, "I'm going to the bathroom" . . . walked out the front door . . . ran to the closest major street . . . called a cab . . . waited on a bus stop bench for it to arrive . . . and took the $75 ride back to my hotel. I'd never been happier to hand anyone $75. Ever.

That's the single riskiest thing I've ever done in my life. Post Breakup Stress Disorder can lead to terrible decisions. This was mine.

---

[222] Between praying for pubic hair and having my life saved here, I've basically used up all of my life's allotment of prayers.

[223] Honestly. Hay. Something was *really* off about this whole night.

This chapter is all about the major dilemmas and problems you may come across in your dating life—from cheating to long-distance relationships to grooming issues to, yes, breakups. These are some of the hardest questions we face, and while these lists can't be tailored to every specific, unique, nuanced situation, we'll hit some of the biggest ones.

At the very least, I hope I can prepare you to handle the big breakup that 99 out of 100 of us have in our 20s, so you don't find yourself in a drunk stranger's car in Vegas careening toward her apartment where her estranged boyfriend may or may not be waiting for you with his brand-new gun.

I already took that (thank God, metaphorical) bullet for you.

11 Signs That Someone Is
Cheating on You

The first time I ever really considered the nuances of cheating was when I heard a song by C+C Music Factory. No, not "Gonna Make You Sweat (Everybody Dance Now)," That song teaches you nothing about cheating (come to think of it, not about sweating either). I learned from a lesser-known song[224] called "Things That Make You Go Hmmm . . ."

In the song, the C+C crew lays out a few different scenarios where all the signs are there that someone's cheating. All those things make you go "hmmm." I consider this list, written a full two decades later, an updated version of "Things That Make You Go Hmmm . . ."—without a sweet, thumping synthesized beat, but with mentions of modern phenomena like cell phones, Debra Messing, and herpes.

(1) No unattended cell phone. Because if that cell phone buzzes with a mysterious phone number or a sensual text message, he/she *needs* to be the one answering it. It's hard to claim "*Just a wrong number*, someone speaking Spanish"[225] when you see a text come in from that same number that says:

"u wanna 8===> ( ) l8r?"

(2) Overcompensating during sex. There's no better way to prove that Everything Is Amazing and Better than Ever and Absolutely Nothing Is Wrong like pulling out every acrobatic,

---

[224] But one that did hit #4 on the charts in 1991.

[225] I'm not sure if this is only an L.A. thing or if it's hit the rest of the United States yet, but in my 9+ years of living here, every single wrong number call I've ever placed or received was someone speaking Spanish.

gymnastic, and superhuman trick in bed. If he/she is normally a straight-missionary-position cold-fish type, then suddenly, one day, *transforms into a sex chimera that's half–Mary Lou Retton, half–one of those Indian guys who can fold himself into a shoebox,* it's worth doing a little investigating.

(3) He/she finally busts out those clothes you bought as a present. You tried really hard to buy him something great and ended up getting an ascot. He swore he liked it, yet for months, maybe years, he never wore it. Then one day, it appears. "I wear it all the time," he insists, "you must not have noticed." You would've noticed. (Any of us would notice a guy wearing an ascot. It's an ascot.)

Sure, there's a chance he's connected with his high-class foppy nobleman side. If he's wearing the ascot while clutching a snifter of brandy and laughing haughtily, you don't have to worry.[226] But it's more likely he's *wearing it out of guilt*—deep down he knows he's wasting your love and affection . . . can't let you waste your money, too.

(4) His/her friends seem uncomfortable around you. It's much easier to catch a vibe off someone's friends than the person him/herself. The friends know what's going on and are in a weird moral gray area—do they act disloyally and betray their friend by telling you about *his/her* disloyalty?[227] Or do they stay loyal to their friend, even though his/her morality is terrible? *It's a very difficult "Would You Rather?" question,* up there with the toughest ones ever, like would you rather get herpes or never eat mustard again?

---

[226] At least—you don't have to worry about cheating. You probably have to worry about this strange shift in his persona.

[227] Do two disloyalties make a loyalty?

Ultimately, most people choose the coward's way out, just acting really distant around you.

(5) Makes a big relationship gesture. The bad news: A surprise trip to Trinidad and/or Tobago quite possibly means cheating is going on (and now, even if it's not, I've planted that seed of doubt in your head like an asshole). The good news: *free trip!*

(6) He/she isn't as affectionate toward your dog. It's not like a dog will use his acute sense of smell to detect the scent of adultery on his/her neck or groin and then report back to you—as of the time of this writing, dogs still can't talk.[228]

But he/she's now carrying a relationship-killing secret on the inside, one that *will certainly cut off all contact with the dog once the secret is inevitably exposed.* And that's just too much to take. To avoid that unbearable separation pain, he/she will start cutting off the dog early.

(7) Constant criticism of a certain type of person. If a guy's cheating on you with a red-haired woman, you better believe the next time you guys are snuggled up watching syndicated *Will & Grace* reruns, he's going to take a break from laughing at Jack and Karen's nonstop zingers and make a comment about how unattractive he finds Debra Messing. It's *an instinctive (albeit mediocre) effort to throw you off the trail*—by talking about how awful redheads are, you'll never suspect he's secretly shacking up with one twice a week in a Red Roof Inn off the interstate.[229]

(8) An empty cell phone call or text log. One hundred percent of the people I know have cell phones. *No one religiously dumps their call or text logs*—not my friends who have billion-

---

[228] Other than Poochie.

[229] You don't have to take a redhead to a Red Roof Inn, by the way. It's not a camouflage thing. It was just a random interstate hotel chain I thought of that happened to have a parallel.

dollar stock secrets, not my friends who work for the government, not my friends who send and receive nude photos with people they met on Adult Friend Finder. So if someone's regularly dumping his/her logs, it's probably because there's something that needs to be hidden.[230]

Also, on that note, if you see a shocking amount of calls or texts to and from an odd source—maybe a name like "Julie" even though you know she doesn't have any friends named Julie, or from "Office Line 3" even though you're not sure why she'd tell the office she "misses your cock" at 1:30 AM on a Saturday—it could be a fake.

(9) Lots of showers. Whether it's to try to eliminate the smell of the other man/woman or it's *some kind of symbolic ritual to wash away the sin,* no one needs to take 37 showers a week. Even prostitutes will sometimes just slap themselves with a moist towelette in between customers.[231]

(10) Asks you to go on a daytime talk show but kinda dances around what the reason is. In college, I interned at *Jerry Springer*, during its heyday. And anytime I'd be in the green room talking to *a guest who wasn't sure why he/she was there, it was a cheating revelation.* And usually a big one, too—I'm cheating with your dad, I'm cheating with a horse, I'm cheating with a pregnant horse, I'm cheating with a pregnant horse's dad. Crazy stuff. Never go on those shows. Never.

(11) A milestone birthday approaching. Ages like 24, 29, 39, 49, 54 . . . these are cheating ages. *People use milestone birthdays as an opportunity to take stock of their lives,* and also use them as moments to make big, sweeping changes when,

---

[230] Upon revision, I realized that I inadvertently used the phrase "dumping his/her logs." Awful.
[231] An unlimited supply of moist towelettes is one of the many perks of being the Special Adviser to the Lieutenant Governor.

inevitably, they're completely disappointed that they're not rock gods or billionaires.[232] So if you suspect cheating, and a major birthday is approaching (or just happened), add that to your "circumstantial evidence" pile. This ain't the legal system. Hearsay and speculation are *totally* in bounds here.

---

[232] This happens no matter how old you get. My grandma just turned 90. She decided to . . . join Netflix.

11 Sensitive Grooming and Body Issues, and How to Address Them

There are right ways and wrong ways to address really sensitive grooming, body, and hygiene issues. For instance, I recently saw my girlfriend had a few dark hairs growing above her lip. Maybe 10 hairs total, which were only visible at a certain angle in a certain light. So perhaps I shouldn't have asked her if she was going to a *Magnum, P.I.* convention, *especially* since I would get absolutely murdered if in a "point out the other's grooming issues" contest.

Of course, the best way to talk to someone about an issue is to just say it directly. But who wants to do *that*, right? Here are strategies to tackle the most uncomfortable personal issues in the most effective, tactful, *and* nonconfrontational ways possible.

(1) Bad breath. Get your point across by *really* playing up the times his/her breath smells good. After he/she's done brushing his/her teeth, eating a mint, chewing some gum—I'd even go as far as to say smoking a menthol cigarette—go in for a kiss. And just rave about how good the kiss is; how much you like his/her breath smelling like that.

Basically, *instead of saying, "You have bad breath" you're saying, "I like you when you have fresh breath."* (You can also transfer that bit of upper-level wordplay over to other occasions. For example, instead of saying, "You're a bad cook," tell him, "I love when you make spaghetti!" If she asks you, "Does my ass look big?" respond, "It looks great *in those pants*." It's really a passive-aggressive catchall.)

(2) Male pubic hair overgrowth. This actually has the easiest, one-sentence solution of all: *"If you trim down there*

I'll go down on you all the time." And then, if he does it, follow through on your promise. Even Pavlov himself couldn't train someone faster.[233]

(3) Female pubic hair overgrowth. Pitch to her that you would love to "try something new." Women want to be perceived as *sexually fun and adventurous,* but don't always know the path (and don't want to have to go *too* far) to achieve that.

This gives her a nice, easy path. In her mind, pubic hair sculpting is a hell of a lot more palatable than installing a sex swing in the ceiling and acting out a full-penetration version of the flying dragon mounting scene from *Avatar*.

(4) Female pubic hair undergrowth. At the time of this writing, the bald look is in. Cultural standards change. If this book ever winds up in a time machine back to the seventies, that's right, foxes—women today actually have more hair on their heads than they do down below. There's even this thing called the Brazilian wax. Back in your time, I believe it was used as a Vietcong torture tactic.

Now, back to talking to modern men. If you prefer that your woman go for that full, Chia retro look (or, more likely, a shapely tuft), just tell her, *"You know what I find sexy? Just a little bit of hair."* Unless she paid thousands of dollars to have everything lasered off, she'll probably prefer not having to bald down every day in the shower.

(5) Male genital odor. Propose a shower together and clean him down there yourself. He'll think he's in the scene from *Coming to America* where the naked women tell Eddie Murphy that "the royal penis is clean." And *every guy wants to be as cool as Eddie Murphy* (at least Eddie Murphy back then).

---

[233] Although I heard he had excellent oral skills.

(6) Female genital odor. The most difficult dilemma on the entire list. It's *very* hard to tackle this directly without looking like a douche bag (pun *fully* intended, by the way).

This advice is raunchy and it's ultra-aggressive. *Since you can't bring her nose to the fight, bring the fight to her nose. So to speak.*

After your fingers have spent some time down there, find a way for them to pass underneath her nose. If things smell as bad as you believe they do, she'll catch the scent. Maybe not this time, but one of these times.[234] Then, once she's added up this evidence and figured out why you are reluctant to head down there—and she responds by making an effort to get everything fresh and clean—go down there with unprecedented passion and vigor.

(7) Male balding. Try this one: "You know how a pregnant woman can't even be in the same building as Propecia because it's too dangerous? *I guess if you start taking it that's a guarantee we won't have a kid anytime soon.*"

(8) Female mustache. This will cost you some money but will be extremely worth it—you want to be dating the Princess, not Mario. Go to her trusted stylist, preferably a blunt, old school Russian woman. Bribe her to whale on your girlfriend or wife about her mustache the next time she's in.

For whatever reason, *women seem to be fine receiving brutal, unfiltered criticism, as long as it's coming from someone they pay to make them look good.* So when she's sitting there getting her hair done and hears, "You, American woman, your lip looks hairy like mine," she'll take the criticism in stride and have that thing waxed right off.

---

[234] Also, make sure you haven't lit any candles in the room there, R. Kelly—you don't want delicious aromatic lavender to drown out the unpleasantness.

(9) Male weight gain. In the list of "11 Signs a Girl's Really Into You" I mentioned that I've known several women who actually celebrate a little male weight gain. It shows he's happy and fed and associating you with delicious food . . . plus it's making him ever so slightly less desirable to random girls.

That being said, when it crosses the line from a few extra pounds to a few extra midnight gravy runs, it might be time to intervene. And there's a nice way to do it and a cruel way to do it.

The nice way: Cook him healthier meals; train together for a half-marathon; and *as soon as he loses any weight compliment the hell out of his body.* The cruel way: Kind of flirt with a guy with a good body. Nothing serious, barely blatant—just enough to tweak the competitiveness in his head that will drive him straight to the gym.

(10) Female weight gain. No man in history has been able to bring up his woman's weight gain smoothly. It's the most vexing topic in the history of mankind. And no matter how much televised puppets may've inflated your young ego, you're not special. *You'll fall into the same trap as everyone else.*

So . . . you should try to address it by changing *your* behavior. If you stop ordering French fries and pie and switch to chicken breasts and salad, she's going to find herself falling into line. She has to. A woman is not going to let herself be the grosser eater in a relationship.[235]

(11) Male fashion choices. I include males and not females here because only a tiny, tiny fraction of men would be able to have grounds to give their wives or girlfriends fashion advice. It would be like a woman giving her husband advice on how to grow a beard.

---

[235] Also, figure out a workout regimen you can do together. That works for two reasons. One, she'll love that she has a workout partner pushing her. And two, she'll love that it's *you*, meaning *you've* proposed a new couples' activity.

Men get fairly set in their ways about their clothes—but can be changed. So find your most fashionable friend (who's also quite attractive) and have her join you two on a trip to a clothing store. Pick a place that sells clothes within his realm of style—if he's still wearing parachute jeans and stonewashed denim shirts with Looney Tunes characters embroidered on the pockets, don't try to get him to wear fine tailored suits or high-fashion patchwork jackets and leg warmers.

You and your friend pick out a bunch of stuff and, as he tries things on and shows them to you, *you both react like you just saw Antonio Sabàto, Jr. himself walk out of that changing room.* Maybe even get the salesgirl on board—she's in it for the sale, so she'll go along with anything—and you guys can triple-team him with compliments. He'll never take those clothes off again.

11 Ways to Transition a Friendship into a Relationship

It's happened a thousand times on a thousand sitcoms. Two longtime friends start feeling that itch for each other . . . after teasing the audience for a while they eventually get together . . . and then the show's ratings start dropping like lightning hit the transmitter. I could use that as a metaphor for how other friends feel when they see two people from their group splinter off into a couple, but I won't—this list is all about the optimism that comes from thinking the love of your life might be the person sitting across the table with lettuce in his teeth.

(1) Make a major change to your look. This friend is used to looking at you. You're not some alluring stranger. You're just a friend. That's right: I say you're just a friend. Want to prove that you got what they need?

Alter the way you look and you can alter the way he/she sees you. A new hairstyle is usually the go-to here; if you want to be the Monica to his Chandler, perhaps try switching to the Rachel?[236]

(2) Casually date other people, carefully. Another way to be seen as a desirable option is to . . . be desired. You don't want to overdo this—if it looks like you're out banging the world, that's going to be an instant turn-off; and if it looks like you're dating one person seriously, that's even worse. But a couple of dates will definitely raise your stock.

---

[236] Or another hairstyle that's been popular in the last 15 years. I hear bangs are something.

This works extra well if you can make those dates with people who are attractive but substance-free. (This means that they have no depth of character, not that they abstain from drugs. That's not really an issue one way or another in this particular situation.) With luck, *the attractiveness will spark a little jealousy* in your friend, but the substance void will provide the assurance that he/she is still a better catch.

(3) Do stuff together without your other friends around. You've hung out a lot in the context of your group of friends, but rarely one-on-one. Find a way to do stuff with just the two of you, so you can *show him/her that you two have your own special chemistry* away from the pack.

Just don't make them seem too much like dates yet. Avoid awkward "did you think we were on a date?" situations by not going to, say, a restaurant where one of you might feel like you have to pick up the bill. Make things more impromptu and casual. *Grabbing* lunch. *Last-minute* movie. *Coincidental* discovery that you both like watching *The Bachelor* and are going to do so every Monday night.[237]

(4) No Lapdog Syndrome. There's a fine line between "I could date him/her" and "I think he/she has a thing for me, and you know what that means: unlimited airport pickups and help when I move!"

Not being eternally available for favors can be more effective than being available for favors all the time. It may not be the nicest way to handle things, and it may go against your instincts, but this way, *you demonstrate how much he/she has grown to miss you when you're not around.*

(5) If you make a move and fail, don't just blame it on the alcohol. When I discussed this list with people, and asked

---

[237] I could've included this in the "11 Signs a Guy's Really Into You" list. He says he likes watching *The Bachelor*? He's into you.

them, "If you started having feelings for your friend, what would you do?" every single person responded with, "Get drunk together and make a move." That's the last time I do interviews at 2 PM on St. Patrick's Day.

All hilarious jokes aside, since this was every person's first instinct, there's clearly *something* there. My thought is this. Yes, alcohol can grease things up nicely and give you that little confidence power-up. But don't hide behind the alcohol; *use it to open the door, not explain why the door's open.*

You've both had drinks—you more than him/her—you go in for a kiss, he/she pulls away, and you suddenly start stammering, "Oh, I'm sorry, I'm so sorry . . . man, I'm really drunk."[238]

Instead, give partial credit to the alcohol, but then recognize that Pandora's box has been opened and you're never going to get a better chance to confess that you have a few feelings. This is your opening to talk about it. And if he/she isn't reciprocating, it's fine— after that aborted kiss things were never going to go back to being perfectly normal anyway.

(6) Test feelings with a kiss, citing *Saved by the Bell* if necessary. I hate to admit it, because it feels like a TV cliché, but sometimes, you really can test if you have feelings for each other by kissing.[239]

If you should get into the conversation about, "We're friends; I don't know if I like you that way or not," try the kiss. It just might reveal what your logical brains can't or won't.

If he/she needs more convincing that a kiss test is the answer, reference the *Saved by the Bell* episode where Zack and Jessie are

---

[238] For reference, see the scene in *Boogie Nights* where Philip Seymour Hoffman tries to kiss Marky Mark. Yes, you also look that awkward. No matter how much you're making him/her feel, feel, feel, feel, feel, feel the heat.

[239] This actually did happen to me once. A friend and I kissed at this party, and things changed in that moment. We danced around it for a few months, then dated for a little while, then had a sloppy breakup, and barely talked again after. I guess you can call that a cautionary tale.

the stars of the school play—*Snow White and the Seven Dorks*, obviously—and are afraid that they have started developing feelings for each other. They kiss and realize nope, just friends. Sure, it was unfortunate that Slater saw them kiss and freaked out about it, but everything worked out in the end. That's what *SbtB* taught us: *You can gauge your feelings with a kiss, and everything always works out in the end.*

(7) Be unpredictably available or unavailable. Instead of trying to win your friend over by constantly being around, creating some separation can be a good thing. It's like the proverb: absence makes the heart grow fonder. Only here, it's more of a situation where *absence makes the heart grow fond initially.* Much less poetic and catchy, but much more tailored to your specific need at this moment.

(8) Don't undermine his/her current relationship. Yes, her boyfriend is terrible, he probably cheats on her, and his name is an eighties movie villain name like Thad or Blaine. Sure, the girl he's dating is a giant harlot who clearly weighs two pounds more than you and has sun-damaged skin.

By pointing that out, you only hurt your case in two major ways: (1) You look like a negative, shit-talking, unsupportive friend, and (2) You might strengthen that awful relationship by *giving them an "us against the world/nothing's gonna stop us now" mentality.*[240] Let your other friends point out all the flaws. You just position yourself to be there when the relationship inevitably implodes.

(9) Find a way to end up sharing a bed. There's something about that private, cuddling supine position that leads to physical escalation. So curl up in a hotel room after a wedding (where you brought him/her as a date), share a tent on a group camping trip,

---

[240] You do *not* want them trying to build this dream together, standing strong forever. Something *should* stop them now. And if not now, then soon.

or stay in a spare bedroom at a party when neither of you can drive home—and suddenly, you may find yourselves going at it.

I don't know why beds bring that out, but I've seen it happen over and over. *It might even be muscle memory,* like how you can take a decade off and still remember how to ride a bike, bowl a 106, or do the Electric Slide.

(10) Hope your other friends start making comments. Your other friends are going to notice—faster than you'd expect them to—that you two are starting to pair off a lot. And they're going to make comments, sometimes in front of both of you together. That's just what friends do.

It may seem uncomfortable at first, especially when he/she instantly responds, "Oh *God* no, nothing's going on, I'd rather kill myself—no offense." Although that kinda hurts your feelings, *it's for the greater good.* Eventually, if it's repeated enough, he/she's going to have to think, "Wait . . . *are* we starting to become a couple?"

(11) Recognize that there's no going back for the friendship. So this is it. If you take *any* action, if you acknowledge these feelings, if you discuss them, if you want to see if you guys really can make it as a couple, the friendship can't ever truly go back. Are you willing to accept that risk?

I'd guess that you are. *If the feelings are real, it's worth it to gamble the friendship on 'em.* The odds say you weren't going to remain friends forever anyway, long term. Just know you may have a *ton* of uncomfortable moments in the short term.

11 Breakup Clichés, and What You Should Say Instead

I put together this breakup primer because of just how incredibly tough it is to break up with someone. (I suppose it's even tougher to be on the receiving end, but at least it doesn't require as much preparation and pain infliction. [Unless someone breaks up with you and you react by stabbing him/her in the shoulder with a fork. (Then it's tough on both ends.)])

(1) "It's not you, it's me." This one's been driven into the ground. We default to it because we hope it'll make our dumpee feel like *we're* the ones with all the relationship-terminating fatal flaws. "Well, there's nothing I could've done," he/she will think, "after all, it wasn't *my* fault."

Even if you genuinely believe this is the truth—it's not, by the way; on some level it *is* him/her, not you—*it's such a generic line that you'll put the other person on the attack.* It'd be like getting into a huge street fight with someone and having him say to you, "You're so ugly, you won't get laid until pigs fly." You're not offended by the insult; you're offended that he *thought* you'd be offended by the insult.

Replacement line: "We want different things." The underlying principle is the same, but this is a more honest angle.

(2) "I love you but I'm not *in* love with you." Suddenly, during a breakup, *everyone becomes a master of the twisted nuances of the English language.* I stay up at night dreaming of **astro**nomically bad puns. So stay off my **turf**.

Replacement line: Instead of playing the semantics game, go the blunter (but more on point), route: "My feelings just aren't as strong as they used to be."[241]

(3) "I don't have time for a relationship." Somehow, whenever someone drops this one, word gets to you two months later that he/she has entered into a brand-new, super-serious relationship. That's because the whole "no time" thing isn't true. *People will make time for a relationship if they want it bad enough.* The president has time for a relationship. Clinton and Kennedy had time for several. You're not busier than those guys. You might not even be busier than Roger Clinton or former MTV VJ Kennedy.

Replacement line: "I'm finding that I'm having a lot of difficulty making our relationship a priority, and I think that's a pretty unmistakable sign."

(4) "You're Mr. Right, not Mr. Right Now." Even a Lifetime Original Movie would reject that line for being too shlocky.[242] You *don't want to be less hip than Lifetime.*

Replacement line: "I know you're a great guy, but I'm just not feeling the chemistry with you."

(5) "We'd be better off as friends." This is garbage because you won't be friends afterward. You just won't. For every relationship where the people break up and stay friends there are 999,999 where *they make a token effort for a while and then never hear from each other again.* It's more difficult than blocking an extra point in a Madden game.[243]

Replacement line: "We still connect great, but I just don't have romantic feelings for you anymore."

---

[241] And then, if you want to lighten the mood, say, "You know, like baseball's power hitters."

[242] I actually believe this line was used un-ironically by Jason Biggs in the movie *My Best Friend's Girl.* I bet at that moment he missed having intercourse with a pie.

[243] Which is really difficult.

(6) "You're perfect and amazing and fantastic, _but_ . . ."
During breakups, we all have this instinct to rattle off a list of 700 positive traits about the person before we drop the bomb. In reality, _that just makes things worse._

Because of the aforementioned bomb at the end, each comment, in retrospect, seems a bit disingenuous. So if you give 15 compliments before the breakup line, that's 15 individual pieces of evidence that you were being disingenuous. And you know what you call someone who's disingenuous 15 times in one conversation? The C-word.[244]

Replacement line: Give just one compliment, and keep it from the subset of words that compliment without overselling. Avoid words like "perfect," "a catch," "a once-in-a-lifetime guy/girl that anyone would be a fool to pass up" . . . and go with words like "great," "sweet," or "cool." You know, really basic, generic stuff.

(7) "I don't deserve you." This might come, at least partially, from a noble place. You're saying: I don't want to clog up your time anymore since I'm a dead end; you need to go find someone who appreciates all you have to offer. Unfortunately, the implication turns out to be: _You've been slumming with me, and now I'm getting rid of you, making you a fool two times over._[245]

Replacement line: "I know I'm not treating you the way you deserve to be treated."

(8) "I'm not attracted to you anymore." This isn't just a cliché, it's a solid way to scar someone for life. Whether you mean it to or not, it implies something changed physically to make him/her less attractive—and that _sets off a whole chain of insecurity dominos._ (Which are like regular dominos, but whinier.)

---

[244] Contemptible.

[245] And like George Bush said, "There's an old saying in Tennessee—I know it's in Texas, probably in Tennessee—that says, fool me once, shame on—[pause]—shame on you. Fool me—[pause]—you can't get fooled again." Chew on that. It started as a proverb and eventually turned into a Who lyric.

Replacement line: "The chemistry here isn't working for me, and I just don't see us going to the next level."

(9) Treating the person like crap until he/she breaks up with you. This was acceptable in middle school. (But so was mixing 10 different kinds of soda into one cup, wearing your braces headgear to school, and bringing a *Family Matters* sleeping bag to sleepovers. Everything evolves.)

Replacement passive-aggressive tactic: If you *must* go this route, just be a little bit distant until you inevitably hear, *"You seem distant. Is something wrong?"* And when that door gets opened, your cowardly ass had better barge through it.

(10) "Deep down I'll always love you." Of course you will. There's no better way to say I love you than completely decimating someone's heart, right? This just feels like mindless sap—*total drivel that can only make someone feel worse.*

Replacement line: None. Just *don't* tack this on to the breakup. This line alone can't get the job done anyway, so just omit it.

(11) "I'm just not that into you." *So played out.*

Replacement line: "The thing is, men are from Mars and women are from Venus."

11 Things You Must Do in Your Single Life before You'll Be Ready to Settle Down

A few jobs ago, I had a coworker named Bob whose dating history I found fascinating. Bob, now in his late 30s, got married to the first and only woman he ever dated, his high school girlfriend. Lifetime, he's had one first date, one sexual partner, one relationship, zero breakups.

I asked Bob dozens of questions, but one stands out in my mind. I asked him if he regretted never having a "single" phase. And, after about three minutes of requisite jokes about different types of women he would've liked to swap fluids with, he gave me the truth. "No," Bob said, "I didn't need it. I found what I was looking for."

Suffice to say, that puts Bob staunchly on one side of the bell curve—the opposite side of Samantha and Tom Jones.

The middle of the curve is the domain for most of us: we want to settle down one day, but definitely want to spend some period of time really experiencing what's out there first. This list is geared toward people in that zone. Not only so you don't spend the rest of your life looking over your shoulder wondering, "What if?" . . . but, when you do meet the right person, you'll know it.

(1) Devote a period of time to going out aggressively. If you're going to be single, you might as well be *single*. Get out there, give lots of people a chance, date against your usual type, go out all the time, call in sick to work, and live it up. If that sounds exhausting, it should. It's completely unsustainable. But for a burst of time, *capitalize on the joy of being young, single, and un-nagged*—and own the dating world. You'll have the next 60 years to sleep and pick out light fixtures.

(2) Get good at sex stuff. No one's a natural. During my first French kiss I thought my face was getting eaten[246]—it took me years and years until I figured out how to assert my kissing style while simultaneously adapting to what a girl was giving me. I could tell a story like that for every one of my "firsts." I honestly don't think I got any good at stuff (beyond breast fondling, at which I was a Yo-Yo Ma–level prodigy) until I was in my mid 20s.

Your single life is a time to hone your craft. You get to *test things out, and learn what works and what doesn't.* You get to learn how to handle situations like farting during sex, people who say unnervingly freaky things, and God's strange decision to make everyone's genitals look similar yet different, like erotic snowflakes. You get experience. You get technique. And you get some fantastic stories.

(3) Date someone who's a different race and/or religion. And this doesn't mean dating a Baptist if you're a Methodist. Under my operating assumption that you're not a racist or religionist, *extend those United Colors of Benetton right on into your dating life.* You'll learn a lot about other people—and, if you're a treacly sentimentalist, about yourself—in the process.[247]

(4) Use condoms. Two reasons: (1) to be safe; and (2) *so you know just how good you're getting it once you're in a committed relationship and don't have to deal with them anymore.*

(5) Have a starter relationship. A bad relationship is actually incredibly good for you. Not at the time, of course—then it's gonna suck—but big picture. When you're young and hop into a

---

[246] It was seventh grade. I'm sure my breath smelled like peanut butter or SpaghettiOs. Or, regrettably, both.

[247] And if that's not enough, you get at least a two-year window of totally absolved race/religion jokes. "I can say white people smell like wet dogs—I dated Thad *and* Blaine!"

relationship, it's probably going to be with someone who's wrong for you. You won't know it at first.[248] But it should become abundantly clear about four or five months in, once you stop hearing beautiful music every time the person talks and, instead, hear all the nonsense he/she's spouting.

And I say, let it ride. Give it time. Get that starter relationship under your belt. And when you break it off, *you'll have a huge list of things that you hated—things you can make sure your next boy/girlfriend doesn't do.*

The best way to figure out what you're looking for in the One is to have a starter relationship with the Completely Wrong One.

(6) Let a really good one get away. During your single life you're going to date a few people who are great and many who are not. They're all going to come and go. You lose interest, or vice versa. You like the person but aren't ready to settle down yet, or vice versa. You see more potential in the relationship than he or she does, or vice versa. You hate all the pastel colors he wears, or (Miami) vice versa.

In one, or many, of those scenarios, a good one is going to get away. Maybe not the perfect one, but a good one. And that's OK. You don't have to lament it forever. Now that you've seen it happen once, *you'll make sure it doesn't happen again.*

(7) Try online dating. There's no guarantee you'll connect with the all people you meet through online dating. Far from it. It's the biggest numbers game. It's the difference between a sniper and Tony Montoya. With regular dating—go out, meet someone, have a conversation, get a number, talk on the phone, make a date—you're a sniper. One bullet. With online dating, you're Scarface, *busting*

---

[248] Even though, at the time, you'll think you know everything there is to know. Then, five years later, you'll look back and say, "Man, I was an *idiot* back then." It happens to everyone. Rod Stewart even has a song about it. And that guy won't just sing about any old thing.

into a room and just showering the place with bullets.
Even if most of them miss, just one of 'em has to hit your target.[249]

(8) Make one very controversial decision. You may read
this as "have a one-night stand with an escaped convict" or "date
someone shorter than me"—we all have different thresholds for
what is and isn't a controversial decision.

But, whether you make one consciously, alcoholically, or accidentally, don't beat yourself up over it. *Making bad decisions
is part of the fun of being single.* And as long as you don't end
up accidentally pregnant, accidentally gonorrhea'd, or accidentally
hacked into bits and shoved into a garbage bag in the truck of a 1969
Pontiac GTO, just roll with it.

(9) Get into the best shape of your life. I say this because
it's about maximizing your single days. I know you have a great
personality. It's worthy of a blue ribbon.[250] But, hit the gym hard
for a few months and *suddenly that personality of yours is
going to appeal to a lot more people.*

It's superficial and shallow and all that. But as long as you're
going to be single, might as well be single and hot.[251] Once you get
into a relationship you can make up for all those missed tuna melts
and hot fudge sundaes. (And then, one day, you two will look at each
other and say, "Holy crap, we've got to fix this," and go on a dual
weight-loss program. It's one of the biggest steps every new couple
takes.)

**(10) Date someone who's thrilling but totally wrong for
you.** I never dated a girl with a million tattoos. I never dated a girl

---

[249] I actually haven't ever seen *Scarface*. But I have seen a lot of MTV *Cribs* and used context
clues from all of the *Scarface* memorabilia owned by the rappers it features to piece together
the basics.

[250] And not just at a county fair. At a state fair. You're that great.

[251] My friend Adam recently dropped at least 40 pounds. His finding? "Suddenly, women find the
stuff I say to be fascinating."

who could arrange/promote/invite me to a threesome. A porn star once gave me her number, and I was too afraid to call and ask her out.[252]

That sentence took me 0.3 seconds to brainstorm because all three of those are on my list of "totally wrong-for-me girls I have a weird thing for." Of course, few people get to cross every item off their list, and I'm not going to get rid of my wonderful girlfriend just so I can have a threesome with a tattooed porn star. But get your kicks in, *fulfill a few random fantasies, and minimize your regrets.*

(Even though I never closed the deal with any of the three women listed above, I did hook up with a few girls who were thrilling but wrong for me, including one who, I'm fairly sure, was a legit anti-Semite. I don't think she realized I was Jewish until it was too late. I sure showed her. I even made up a word to describe the situation: circumsurprised.)

(11) Date enough people to realize the qualities you thought you wanted were all wrong. In your head, you probably have a list of qualities you're looking for in your future husband or wife.[253]

When you've had a strong single phase—some mini-relationships, several terrible first dates, some random hookups—two things

---

[252] This was in January 2009 when I was working as an on-camera host and doing a video segment at the Adult Entertainment Expo. I'd just interviewed a red-haired porn star—I know her name, and I'll tell you if you ask—and, once the camera was off, she and I started talking for real. We hit it off, she told me her real name and age, and we talked about hanging out back in L.A. She gave me her number. I never called. Let's say it was because I had just met the girl who's now my girlfriend and not because I'm a coward. (And no, I don't have the number anymore. Let's say it's because I deleted it out of respect to my girlfriend and not that it was gone forever when my phone got stolen at the gym about nine months ago.)

[253] Some people actually go as far as to write this list down. That always struck me as a bit much, but people do it. One of my friends even kept the list in his wallet. . . . I guess in case he needed to size someone up on the go. That seems extreme.

should become clear: (1) *There's no such thing as a person who has every little quality that you're looking for;* (2) and even if that person did exist, just because he/she has all the qualities you want on paper, that doesn't mean you're going to have that once-in-a-lifetime connection.

I could've given you a spoiler alert for this—it's the revelation that everyone has. And once you have it, whether you realize it or not, *now* you're truly ready to enter into a serious relationship.

Of course, there's the other side of the coin, too: If you have that revelation, kick your single life into *overdrive* and get everything out of your system quick. 'Cause the end is near. In a totally wonderful, blessed, emotionally fulfilling way. But still, the end.

11 Keys to Pulling off a
Long-Distance Relationship

Everyone who's in a short-distance relationship says the same thing to their friends in long-distance relationships: "Man, I just don't know how you do it." The truth is, it's not *that* mind boggling, like some kind of magic trick where a woman gets sawed into four parts and then four monkeys jump out of the boxes. It just takes faith, patience, and the confidence to strip down in front of a computer. And money for travel. Lots and lots and lots of money for travel.

(1) Set a date when the long distance will end, or you will fail. You can't be long distance forever. At some point, one of you is going to have to pick up and move. And if you know that date is coming, it's easy to hold on. In six months, 12 months, two years, whatever—as long as you both know there's a definite point in the future where you'll be in a short-distance relationship, you can grow as a couple.

The problems start when things are indefinite. No one's willing to flinch on the moving thing and hope erodes, until one day you give up.[254]

(2) Drastically reduce your solo vacations. When you enter into a long-distance relationship, you're signing a contract that says, "I now know where 100 percent of my vacation time will be allotted." *Your trips are now exclusively focused on getting together with him/her.* Sorry.

---

[254] And you don't want hope to erode, you want hope to float. Like in the movie *Hope Floats*. Remember what happened there? Sandra Bullock ditched her long-distance relationship for a short-distance relationship. At least according to Wikipedia.

(If you want to travel solo, you've got to use your sick days, although it's hard to get away with the "[cough] I'm feeling really sick I think I'm going to go to the doctor and won't be in today [cough]" phone call to your boss when the caller ID comes up with India's country code.[255])

(3) Don't always meet up in each other's cities. Instead of always visiting him where he lives or visiting her where she lives, go on a vacation together in between. If you don't, *you'll somehow find monotony in your infrequent, brief, passionate get-togethers*—and that ain't right.

Also, by meeting in between, you both can still use your vacation days for more exotic vacations. Even if by "exotic" that means "meeting in Clearwater, Florida."

(4) You don't necessarily have to talk on the phone every night. It's kind of counterintuitive, but the demise of long-distance phone charges may have changed long-distance relationships for the worse.

It's hard to remember these days, but, back in that mythical period before this century started, long-distance calls were expensive. When you talked to someone in another city, you made every word count because you could quantify those words into actual dollars. Now it doesn't matter—you can sit there in silence for three hours as long as it's after 9 PM or a weekend. Talk has become cheap. In two ways.

So . . . while you should have some kind of contact every single day (text, instant message, whatever), *nightly phone calls will eventually drag you both down.*

"How was your day?"

"Fine. Yours?"

---

[255] The "[cough] I'm feeling really sick" call is the business world's equivalent of the "um . . . thing."

"Fine."

[fight]

When the calls become a strangely repetitive chore, that's when you *really* start resenting the long-distance relationship.

(5) You should, however, check in before you go to bed on weekend nights. During the week you're distracted with work and tiredness and very important reality shows. On the weekends, when you're alone in your bedroom—your friends are all with their significant others or less significant randoms, and you start looking online just to see how much it might cost to get a cat—*that's when the long-distance separation hits.* So check in to say four things: (1) I'm alive; (2) I miss you, too; (3) No, I'm not cheating on you right now; and (4) I just came dangerously close to getting a cat.[256]

(6) Learn the finer points of phone sex. There are many different approaches here for people of all comfort levels. On one end of things, there's the occasional dirty text message. On the other end, there's getting naked on Skype and having one person remotely control the other's sex toy that was actually custom-made from a mold of their genitalia.[257] There's an entire spectrum in between to choose from, but, no matter what, you've got to choose something. You don't get to make actual physical contact on a regular basis. *At least you can fondle each other's minds.*

---

[256] Or, quite possibly, *another* cat.

[257] You actually can get a sex toy made out of a mold of your stuff. They sell kits on the Internet. I assume it works like when you'd go to the dentist or orthodontist and he'd have you bite down on two metal sheets filled with flavored paste to make a perfect mold of your teeth. Of course, these days, I've heard you can skip all that and just make computer models of your mouth. Ridiculous. I swear, if they eradicate braces by the time my kids need them, I'm going to make them get the old-fashioned kind for a few years anyway. It builds character. You learn really quickly how to have a good personality when you've got braces.

(7) Don't freak out if you get together in person and start arguing. I could armchair psychologist this up all day, but, for whatever reason, I've seen that people in long-distance relationships tend to get into arguments during their time face-to-face.

Just know it's part of the deal, and *you can silence the alarm in your head* going "Oh my God, we'll never get along if we live in the same place all we do is fight." Well . . . you probably can't fully silence it. But you can hit the snooze button on it (which should last until your next face-to-face fight).

(8) Put an extra emphasis on birthdays and holidays. Being together for big events like birthdays, holidays, graduations, or parole hearings is important. In fact, *spending those tent pole moments together can compensate for a lot of time apart.* That way, when you look at photos or think back on the big occasions, he/she will be there—and seem like he/she's *always* there.

So be there for his birthday, go home to her family on Thanksgiving, surprise him for his graduation, and bake a cake with a file inside to take to his parole hearing.

(9) Lots of short visits are better than a few long ones. In a long-distance situation, the really lengthy stretches apart are the ones that weigh on you the most—especially when you don't have another visit scheduled. So if you get 15 vacation days from work—and you can afford to make a lot of trips—why not take 15 Fridays off? Plus, *if you're together for shorter periods, you can completely focus on each other* without pain-in-the-ass life getting in the way; if you visit for two weeks, he/she's going to have to go to work, do laundry, run errands, and wash dishes for at least some of it.